This book has been published by:

Contact: sales@nuvisionpublications.com

URL: http://www.nuvisionpublications.com

Publishing Date: 2008

ISBN# 1-59547-577-X

Please see our website for several books created for
education, research and entertainment.

Specializing in rare, out-of-print books still in demand.

NuVision Publications, LLC is dedicated to bringing new life to rare, historic, and formerly out-of-print books. Most re-print publishers simply photocopy, or scan and print the pages from the original book, which can make the book hard to read as most re-print books are 100+ years old. It is our policy to take the time to convert the original faded, sometimes blotched text into crisp, clear digital text. <u>All</u> of our printed books have been completely reformatted to be easy to read and enjoy.

Please note that we do not correct out-of-date facts or grammar-type errors that were in the original book. We do our best to retain the original composition of the text, the way the author intended it.

NuVision Publications, LLC
Sioux Falls, SD USA

LOMBARD STREET

A Description of the Money Market.

By WALTER BAGEHOT

1897

Table of Contents

CHAPTER I

Introductory

I venture to call this Essay 'Lombard Street,' and not the 'Money Market,' or any such phrase, because I wish to deal, and to show that I mean to deal, with concrete realities. A notion prevails that the Money Market is something so impalpable that it can only be spoken of in very abstract words, and that therefore books on it must always be exceedingly difficult. But I maintain that the Money Market is as concrete and real as anything else; that it can be described in as plain words; that it is the writer's fault if what he says is not clear. In one respect, however, I admit that I am about to take perhaps an unfair advantage. Half, and more than half, of the supposed 'difficulty' of the Money Market has arisen out of the controversies as to 'Peel's Act,' and the abstract discussions on the theory on which that act is based, or supposed to be based. But in the ensuing pages I mean to speak as little as I can of the Act of 1844; and when I do speak of it, I shall deal nearly exclusively with its experienced effects, and scarcely at all, if at all, with its refined basis.

For this I have several reasons,--one, that if you say anything about the Act of 1844, it is little matter what else you say, for few will attend to it. Most critics will seize on the passage as to the Act, either to attack it or defend it, as if it were the main point. There has been so much fierce controversy as to this Act of Parliament--and there is still so much animosity--that a single sentence respecting it is far more interesting to very many than a whole book on any other part of the subject. Two hosts of eager disputants on this subject ask of every new writer the one question--Are you with us or against us? and they care for little else. Of course if the Act of 1844 really were, as is commonly thought, the primum mobile of the English Money Market, the source of all good according to some, and the source of all harm according to others, the extreme irritation excited by an opinion on it would be no reason for not giving a free opinion. A writer on any subject must not neglect its cardinal fact, for fear that others may abuse him. But, in my judgment, the Act of 1844 is only a subordinate matter in the Money Market; what has to be said on it has been said at disproportionate length; the phenomena connected with it have been magnified into greater relative importance than they at all deserve. We must never forget that a quarter of a century has passed since 1844, a period singularly remarkable for its material progress, and almost marvellous in its banking development. Even, therefore, if the facts so much referred to in 1844 had the importance then ascribed to them, and I believe that in some respects they were even then overstated, there would be nothing surprising in finding that in a new world new phenomena had arisen which now are larger and stronger. In my opinion this is the truth: since 1844, Lombard Street is so changed that we cannot judge of it without describing and discussing a most vigorous adult world which then was small and weak. On this account I wish to say as little as is fairly possible of the Act of 1844, and, as far as I can, to isolate and dwell exclusively on the 'Post-Peel' agencies, so that those who have had enough of that well-worn theme (and they are very many) may not be wearied, and that the new and neglected parts of the subject may be seen as they really are.

The briefest and truest way of describing Lombard Street is to say that it is by far the greatest combination of economical power and economical delicacy that the world has even seen. Of the greatness of the power there will be no doubt. Money is economical power. Everyone is aware that England is the greatest moneyed country in the world; everyone admits that it has much more immediately disposable and ready cash than any other country. But very few persons are aware how much greater the ready balance--the floating loan-fund which can be lent to anyone or for any purposeis in England than it is anywhere else in the world. A very few figures will show how large the London loan-fund is, and how much greater it is than any other. The known deposits--the deposits of banks which publish their accounts--are, in

London (31st December, ...1872) 120,000,000 L
Paris (27th February, ...1873) 13,000,000 L
New York (February, ...1873) 40,000,000 L
German Empire (31st January, ...1873) 8,000,000 L

And the unknown deposits--the deposits in banks which do not publish their accounts--are in London much greater than those many other of these cities. The bankers' deposits of London are many times greater than those of any other city--those of Great Britain many times greater than those of any other country.

Of course the deposits of bankers are not a strictly accurate measure of the resources of a Money Market. On the contrary, much more cash exists out of banks in France and Germany, and in all non-banking countries, than could be found in England or Scotland, where banking is developed. But that cash is not, so to speak, 'money-market money:' it is not attainable. Nothing but their immense misfortunes, nothing but a

8

vast loan in their own securities, could have extracted the hoards of France from the custody of the French people. The offer of no other securities would have tempted them, for they had confidence in no other securities. For all other purposes the money hoarded was useless and might as well not have been hoarded. But the English money is 'borrowable' money. Our people are bolder in dealing with their money than any continental nation, and even if they were not bolder, the mere fact that their money is deposited in a bank makes it far more obtainable. A million in the hands of a single banker is a great power; he can at once lend it where he will, and borrowers can come to him, because they know or believe that he has it. But the same sum scattered in tens and fifties through a whole nation is no power at all: no one knows where to find it or whom to ask for it. Concentration of money in banks, though not the sole cause, is the principal cause which has made the Money Market of England so exceedingly rich, so much beyond that of other countries.

The effect is seen constantly. We are asked to lend, and do lend, vast sums, which it would be impossible to obtain elsewhere. It is sometimes said that any foreign country can borrow in Lombard Street at a price: some countries can borrow much cheaper than others; but all, it is said, can have some money if they choose to pay enough for it. Perhaps this is an exaggeration; but confined, as of course it was meant to be, to civilised Governments, it is not much of an exaggeration. There are very few civilised Governments that could not borrow considerable sums of us if they choose, and most of them seem more and more likely to choose. If any nation wants even to make a railway--especially at all a poor nation--it is sure to come to this country--to the country of banks-- for the money. It is true that English bankers are not themselves very great lenders to foreign states. But they are great lenders to those who lend. They advance on foreign stocks, as the phrase is, with 'a margin;' that is, they find eighty per cent of the money, and the nominal lender finds the rest. And it is in this way that vast works are achieved with English aid which but for that aid would never have been planned.

In domestic enterprises it is the same. We have entirely lost the idea that any undertaking likely to pay, and seen to be likely, can perish for want of money; yet no idea was more familiar to our ancestors, or is more common now in most countries. A citizen of London in Queen Elizabeth's time could not have imagined our state of mind. He would have thought that it was of no use inventing railways (if he could have understood what a railway meant), for you would not have been able to collect the capital with which to make them. At this moment, in colonies and all rude countries, there is no large sum of transferable money; there is no fund from which you can borrow, and out of which you can make immense works. Taking the world as a whole--either now or in the past--it is certain that in poor states there is no spare money for new and great undertakings, and that in most rich states the money is too scattered, and clings too close to the hands of the owners, to be often obtainable in large quantities for new purposes. A place like Lombard

Street, where in all but the rarest times money can be always obtained upon good security or upon decent prospects of probable gain, is a luxury which no country has ever enjoyed with even comparable equality before.

But though these occasional loans to new enterprises and foreign States are the most conspicuous instances of the power of Lombard Street, they are not by any means the most remarkable or the most important use of that power. English trade is carried on upon borrowed capital to an extent of which few foreigners have an idea, and none of our ancestors could have conceived. In every district small traders have arisen, who 'discount their bills' largely, and with the capital so borrowed, harass and press upon, if they do not eradicate, the old capitalist. The new trader has obviously an immense advantage in the struggle of trade. If a merchant have 50,000 L. all his own, to gain 10 per cent on it he must make 5,000 l. a year, and must charge for his goods accordingly; but if another has only 10,000 L., and borrows 40,000 L. by discounts (no extreme instance in our modem trade), he has the same capital of 50,000 L. to use, and can sell much cheaper. If the rate at which he borrows be 5 per cent., he will have to pay 2,000 L. a year; and if, like the old trader, he make 5,000 L. a year, he will still, after paying his interest, obtain 3,000 L. a year, or 30 per cent, on his own 10,000 L. As most merchants are content with much less than 30 per cent, he will be able, if he wishes, to forego some of that profit, lower the price of the commodity, and drive the old-fashioned trader-- the man who trades on his own capital--out of the market. In modem English business, owing to the certainty of obtaining loans on discount of bills or otherwise at a moderate rate of interest, there is a steady bounty on trading with borrowed capital, and a constant discouragement to confine yourself solely or mainly to your own capital.

This increasingly democratic structure of English commerce is very unpopular in many quarters, and its effects are no doubt exceedingly mixed. On the one hand, it prevents the long duration of great families of merchant princes, such as those of Venice and Genoa, who inherited nice cultivation as well as great wealth, and who, to some extent, combined the tastes of an aristocracy with the insight and verve of men of business. These are pushed out, so to say, by the dirty crowd of little men. After a generation or two they retire into idle luxury. Upon their immense capital they can only obtain low profits, and these they do not think enough to compensate them for the rough companions and rude manners they must meet in business. This constant levelling of our commercial houses is, too, unfavourable to commercial morality. Great firms, with a reputation which they have received from the past, and which they wish to transmit to the future, cannot be guilty of small frauds. They live by a continuity of trade, which detected fraud would spoil. When we scrutinise the reason of the impaired reputation of English goods, we find it is the fault of new men with little money of their own, created by bank 'discounts.' These men want business at once, and they produce an inferior article to get it. They rely on cheapness, and rely successfully.

But these defects and others in the democratic structure of commerce are compensated by one great excellence. No country of great hereditary trade, no European country at least, was ever so little 'sleepy,' to use the only fit word, as England; no other was ever so prompt at once to seize new advantages. A country dependent mainly on great 'merchant princes' will never be so prompt; their commerce perpetually slips more and more into a commerce of routine. A man of large wealth, however intelligent, always thinks, more or less 'I have a great income, and I want to keep it. If things go on as they are I shall certainly keep it; but if they change I may not keep it.' Consequently he considers every change of circumstance a 'bore,' and thinks of such changes as little as he can. But a new man, who has his way to make in the world, knows that such changes are his opportunities; he is always on the look-out for them, and always heeds them when he finds them. The rough and vulgar structure of English commerce is the secret of its life; for it contains 'the propensity to variation,' which, in the social as in the animal kingdom, is the principle of progress.

In this constant and chronic borrowing, Lombard Street is the great go-between. It is a sort of standing broker between quiet saving districts of the country and the active employing districts. Why particular trades settled in particular places it is often difficult to say; but one thing is certain, that when a trade has settled in any one spot, it is very difficult for another to oust it--impossible unless the second place possesses some very great intrinsic advantage. Commerce is curiously conservative in its homes, unless it is imperiously obliged to migrate. Partly from this cause, and partly from others, there are whole districts in England which cannot and do not employ their own money. No purely agricultural county does so. The savings of a county with good land but no manufactures and no trade much exceed what can be safely lent in the county. These savings are first lodged in the local banks, are by them sent to London, and are deposited with London bankers, or with the bill brokers. In either case the result is the same. The money thus sent up from the accumulating districts is employed in discounting the bills of the industrial districts. Deposits are made with the bankers and bill brokers in Lombard Street by the bankers of such counties as Somersetshire and Hampshire, and those bill brokers and bankers employ them in the discount of bills from Yorkshire and Lancashire. Lombard Street is thus a perpetual agent between the two great divisions of England, between the rapidly-growing districts, where almost any amount of money can be well and easily employed, and the stationary and the declining districts, where there is more money than can be used.

This organisation is so useful because it is so easily adjusted. Political economists say that capital sets towards the most profitable trades, and that it rapidly leaves the less profitable and non-paying trades. But in ordinary countries this is a slow process, and some persons who want to have ocular demonstration of abstract truths have been inclined to doubt it because they could not see it. In England, however, the process would be visible enough if you could only see the books of the bill brokers and the bankers. Their bill cases as a rule are full of the bills drawn in the most profitable trades, and *caeteris paribus* and in comparison empty of those drawn in the less profitable. If the iron trade ceases to be as profitable as usual, less iron is sold; the fewer the sales the fewer the bills; and in consequence the number of iron bills in Lombard street is diminished. On the other hand, if in consequence of a bad harvest the corn trade becomes on a sudden profitable, immediately 'corn bills' are created in great numbers, and if good are discounted in Lombard Street. Thus English capital runs as surely and instantly where it is most wanted, and where there is most to be made of it, as water runs to find its level.

This efficient and instantly-ready organisation gives us an enormous advantage in competition with less advanced countries--less advanced, that is, in this particular respect of credit. In a new trade English capital is instantly at the disposal of persons capable of understanding the new opportunities and of making good use of them. In countries where there is little money to lend, and where that little is lent tardily and reluctantly, enterprising traders are long kept back, because they cannot at once borrow the capital, without which skill and knowledge are useless. All sudden trades come to England, and in so doing often disappoint both rational probability and the predictions of philosophers. The Suez Canal is a curious case of this. All predicted that the canal would undo what the discovery of the passage to India round the Cape effected. Before that all Oriental trade went to ports in the South of Europe, and was thence diffused through Europe. That London and Liverpool should be centres of East Indian commerce is a geographical anomaly, which the Suez Canal, it was said, would rectify. 'The Greeks,' said M. de Tocqueville, 'the Styrians, the Italians, the Dalmatians, and the Sicilians, are the people who will use the Canal if any use it.' But, on the contrary, the main use of the Canal has been by the English. None of the nations named by Tocqueville had the capital, or a tithe of it, ready to build the large screw steamers which alone can use the Canal profitably. Ultimately these plausible predictions may or may not be right, but as yet they have been quite wrong, not because England has rich people--there are wealthy people in all countries--but because she possesses an unequalled fund of floating money, which will help in a moment any merchant who sees a great prospect of new profit.

And not only does this unconscious 'organisation of capital,' to use a continental phrase, make the English specially quick in comparison with their neighbours on the continent at seizing on novel mercantile opportunities, but it makes them likely also to retain any trade on which they have once regularly fastened. Mr. Macculloch, following Ricardo, used to teach that all old nations had a special aptitude for trades in which much capital is required. The interest of capital having been reduced in such countries, he argued, by the necessity of continually resorting to inferior soils, they can undersell countries where profit is high in all trades needing great capital. And in this theory there is doubtless much truth, though it can only be applied in practice after a number of limitations and with a number of deductions of which the older school of political economists did not take enough notice. But the same principle plainly and practically applies to England, in consequence of her habitual use of borrowed capital. As has been explained, a new man, with a small capital of his own and a large borrowed capital, can undersell a rich man who depends on his own capital only. The rich man wants the full rate of mercantile profit on the whole of the capital employed in his trade, but the poor man wants only the interest of money (perhaps not a third of the rate of profit) on very much of what he uses, and therefore an income will be an ample recompense to the poor man which would starve the rich man out of the trade. All the common notions about the new competition of foreign countries with England and its dangersnotions in which there is in other aspects much truth require to be reconsidered in relation to this aspect. England has a special machinery for getting into trade new men who will be content with low prices, and this machinery will probably secure her success, for no other country is soon likely to rival it effectually.

There are many other points which might be insisted on, but it would be tedious and useless to elaborate the picture. The main conclusion is very plainthat English trade is become essentially a trade on borrowed capital, and that it is only by this refinement of our banking system that we are able to do the sort of trade we do, or to get through the quantity of it.

But in exact proportion to the power of this system is its delicacy I should hardly say too much if I said its danger. Only our familiarity blinds us to the marvellous nature of the system. There never was so much borrowed money collected in the world as is now collected in London. Of the many millions in Lombard street, infinitely the greater proportion is held by bankers or others on short notice or on demand; that is to say, the owners could ask for it all any day they please: in a panic some of them do ask for some of it. If any large fraction of that money really was demanded, our banking system and our industrial system too would be in great danger.

Some of those deposits too are of a peculiar and very distinct nature. Since the Franco-German war, we have become to a much larger extent than before the Bankers of Europe. A very large sum of foreign money is on various accounts and for various purposes held here. And in a time of panic it might be asked for. In 1866 we held only a much smaller sum of foreign money, but that smaller sum was demanded and we had to pay it at great cost and suffering, and it would be far worse if we had to pay the greater sums we now hold, without better resources than we had then.

It may be replied, that though our instant liabilities are great, our present means are large; that though we have much we may be asked to pay at any moment, we have very much always ready to pay it with. But, on the contrary, there is no country at present, and there never was any country before, in which the ratio of the cash reserve to the bank deposits was so small as it is now in England. So far from our being able to rely on the proportional magnitude of our cash in hand, the amount of that cash is so exceedingly small that a bystander almost trembles when he compares its minuteness with the immensity of the credit which rests upon it.

Again, it may be said that we need not be alarmed at the magnitude of our credit system or at its refinement, for that we have learned by experience the way of controlling it, and always manage it with discretion. But we do not always manage it with discretion. There is the astounding instance of Overend, Gurney, and Co. to the contrary. Ten years ago that house stood next to the Bank of England in the City of London; it was better known abroad than any similar firm known, perhaps, better than any purely English firm. The partners had great estates, which had mostly been made in the business. They still derived an immense income from it. Yet in six years they lost all their own wealth, sold the business to the company, and then lost a large part of the company's capital. And these losses were made in a manner so reckless and so foolish, that one would think a child who had lent money in the City of London would have lent it better. After this example, we must not confide too surely in long-established credit, or in firmly-rooted traditions of business. We must examine the system on which these great masses of money are manipulated, and assure ourselves that it is safe and right.

But it is not easy to rouse men of business to the task. They let the tide of business float before them; they make money or strive to do so while it passes, and they are unwilling to think where it is going. Even the great collapse of Overends, though it caused a panic, is beginning to be forgotten. Most men of business think'Anyhow this system will probably last my time. It has gone on a long time, and is likely to go on still.' But the exact point is, that it has not gone on a long time. The collection of these immense sums in one place and in few hands is perfectly new. In 1844 the liabilities of the four great London Joint Stock Banks were 10,637,000 L.; they now are more than 60,000,000 L. The private deposits of the Bank of England then were 9,000,000 L.; they now are 8,000,000 L. There was in throughout the country but a fraction of the vast deposit business which now exists. We cannot appeal, therefore, to experience to prove the safety of our system as it now is, for the present magnitude of that system is entirely new. Obviously a system may be fit to regulate a few millions, and yet quite inadequate when it is set to cope with many millions. And thus it may be with 'Lombard Street,' so rapid has been its growth, and so unprecedented is its nature.

I am by no means an alarmist. I believe that our system, though curious and peculiar, may be worked safely; but if we wish so to work it, we must study it. We must not think we have an easy task when we have a difficult task, or that we are living in a natural state when we are really living in an artificial one. Money will not manage itself, and Lombard street has a great deal of money to manage.

CHAPTER II.

A General View of Lombard Street.

I.

The objects which you see in Lombard Street, and in that money world which is grouped about it, are the Bank of England, the Private Banks, the Joint Stock Banks, and the bill brokers. But before describing each of these separately we must look at what all have in common, and at the relation of each to the others.

The distinctive function of the banker, says Ricardo, 'begins as soon as he uses the money of others;' as long as he uses his own money he is only a capitalist. Accordingly all the banks in Lombard Street (and bill brokers are for this purpose only a kind of bankers) hold much money belonging to other people on running account and on deposit. In continental language, Lombard Street is an organization of credit, and we are to see if it is a good or bad organization in its kind, or if, as is most likely, it turn out to be mixed, what are its merits and what are its defects?

The main point on which one system of credit differs from another is 'soundness.' Credit means that a certain confidence is given, and a certain trust reposed. Is that trust justified? and is that confidence wise? These are the cardinal questions. To put it more simplycredit is a set of promises to pay; will those promises be kept? Especially in banking, where the 'liabilities,' or promises to pay, are so large, and the time at which to pay them, if exacted, is so short, an instant capacity to meet engagements is the cardinal excellence.

All which a banker wants to pay his creditors is a sufficient supply of the legal tender of the country, no matter what that legal tender may be. Different countries differ in their laws of legal tender, but for the primary purposes of banking these systems are not material. A good system of currency will benefit the country, and a bad system will hurt it. Indirectly, bankers will be benefited or injured with the country in which they live; but practically, and for the purposes of their daily life, they have no need to think, and never do think, on theories of currency. They look at the matter simply. They say 'I am under an obligation to pay such and such sums of legal currency; how much have I in my till, or have I at once under my command, of that currency?' In America, for example, it is quite enough for a banker to hold 'greenbacks,' though the value of these changes as the Government chooses to enlarge or contract the issue. But a practical New York banker has no need to think of the goodness or badness of this system at all; he need only keep enough 'greenbacks' to pay all probable demands, and then he is fairly safe from the risk of failure.

By the law of England the legal tenders are gold and silver coin (the last for small amounts only), and Bank of England notes. But the number of our attainable bank notes is not, like American 'greenbacks,' dependent on the will of the State; it is limited by the provisions of the Act of 1844. That Act separates the Bank of England into two halves. The Issue Department only issues notes, and can only issue 15,000,000 L. on Government securities; for all the rest it must have bullion deposited. Take, for example an account, which may be considered an average specimen of those of the last few years--that for the last week of 1869:

An account pursuant to the Act 7th and 8th Victoria, cap. 32, for the week ending on Wednesday, the 29th day of December, 1869.

ISSUE DEPARTMENT.

Notes issued 33,288,640 L	Government debt	11,015,100 L
	Other securities	3,984,900 L
	Gold coin and bullion	18,288,640 L
	Silver bullion	
33,288,640		33,288,640 L

BANKING DEPARTMENT.

Proprietors' capital	14,553,000 L	Government Securities	13,811,953 L
Rest	3,103,301 L	Other securities	19,781,988 L
Public deposits,		Notes	10,389,690 L
including Exchequer,		Gold and silver coins	907,982 L
Savings' Banks,			
Commissioners of			
National Debt,			
and dividend			
accounts	8,585,215 L		
Other deposits	18,204,607 L		
Seven-day and other			
bills	445,490 L		44,891,613 L
44,891,613 L			

GEO. FORBES, Chief Cashier.

Dated the 30th December, 1869.

There are here 15,000,000 L. bank notes issued on securities, and 18,288,640 L. represented by bullion. The Bank of England has no power by law to increase the currency in any other manner. It holds the stipulated amount of securities, and for all the rest it must have bullion. This is the 'cast iron' system—the 'hard and fast' line which the opponents of the Act say ruins us, and which the partizans of the Act say saves us. But I have nothing to do with its expediency here. All which is to my purpose is that our paper 'legal tender,' our bank notes, can only be obtained in this manner. If, therefore, an English banker retains a sum of Bank of England notes or coin in due proportion to his liabilities, he has a sufficient amount of the legal tender of this country, and he need not think of anything more.

But here a distinction must be made. It is to be observed that properly speaking we should not include in the 'reserve' of a bank 'legal tenders,' or cash, which the Bank keeps to transact its daily business. That is as much a part of its daily stock-in-trade as its desks or offices; or at any rate, whatever words we may choose to use, we must carefully distinguish between this cash in the till which is wanted every day, and the safety-fund, as we may call it, the special reserve held by the bank to meet extraordinary and unfrequent demands.

What then, subject to this preliminary explanation, is the amount of legal tender held by our bankers against their liabilities? The answer is remarkable, and is the key to our whole system. It may be broadly said that no bank in London or out of it holds any considerable sum in hard cash or legal tender (above what is wanted for its daily business) except the Banking Department of the Bank of England. That department had on the 29th day of December, 1869, liabilities as follows:

Public deposits	8,585,000 L
Private deposits	18,205,000 L
Seven-day and other bills	445,000 L
Total	27,235,000 L

and a cash reserve of 11,297,000 L. And this is all the cash reserve, we must carefully remember, which, under the law, the Banking Department of the Bank of England--as we cumbrously call it the Bank of England for banking purposes--possesses. That department can no more multiply or manufacture bank notes than any other bank can multiply them. At that particular day the Bank of England had only 11,297,000 L. in its till against liabilities of nearly three times the amount. It had 'Consols' and other securities which it could offer for sale no doubt, and which, if sold, would augment its supply of bank notesand the relation of such securities to real cash will be discussed presently; but of real cash, the Bank of England for this purpose--the banking bank--had then so much and no more.

And we may well think this a great deal, if we examine the position of other banks. No other bank holds any amount of substantial importance in its own till beyond what is wanted for daily purposes. All London banks keep their principal reserve on deposit at the Banking Department of the Bank of England. This is by far the easiest and safest place for them to use. The Bank of England thus has the responsibility of taking care of it. The same reasons which make it desirable for a private person to keep a banker make it also desirable for every banker, as respects his reserve, to bank with another banker if he safely can. The custody of very large sums in solid cash entails much care, and some cost; everyone wishes to shift these upon others if he can do so without suffering. Accordingly, the other bankers of London, having perfect confidence in the Bank of England, get that bank to keep their reserve for them.

The London bill brokers do much the same. Indeed, they are only a special sort of bankers who allow daily interest on deposits, and who for most of their money give security. But we have no concern now with these differences of detail. The bill brokers lend most of their money, and deposit the remnant either with the Bank of England or some London banker. That London banker lends what he chooses of it, the rest he leaves at the Bank of England. You always come back to the Bank of England at last. But those who keep immense sums with a banker gain a convenience at the expense of a danger. They are liable to lose them if the bank fail. As all other bankers keep their banking reserve at the Bank of England, they are liable to fail if it fails. They are dependent on the management of the Bank of England in a day of difficulty and at a crisis for the spare money they keep to meet that difficulty and crisis. And in this there is certainly considerable risk. Three times 'Peel's Act' has been suspended because the Banking Department was empty. Before the Act was broken--

In 1847, the Banking Department was reduced to L 1,994,000
1857 " " L 1,462,000
1866 " " L 3,000,000

In fact, in none of those years could the Banking Department of the Bank of England have survived if the law had not been broken. Nor must it be fancied that this danger is unreal, artificial, and created by law. There is a risk of our thinking so, because we hear that the danger can be cured by breaking an Act; but substantially the same danger existed before the Act. In 1825, when only coin was a legal tender, and when there was only one department in the Bank, the Bank had reduced its reserve to 1,027,000 L., and was within an ace of stopping payment.

But the danger to the depositing banks is not the sole or the principal consequence of this mode of keeping the London reserve. The main effect is to cause the reserve to be much smaller in proportion to the liabilities than it would otherwise be. The reserve of the London bankers being on deposit in the Bank of England, the Bank always lends a principal part of it. Suppose, a favourable supposition, that the Banking Department holds more than two-fifths of its liabilities in cashthat it lends three-fifths of its deposits and retains in reserve only two-fifths. If then the aggregate of the bankers' deposited reserve be 5,000,000 L., 3,000,000 L. of it will be lent by the Banking Department, and 2,000,000 L. will be kept in the till. In consequence, that 2,000,000 L. is all which is really held in actual cash as against the liabilities of the depositing banks. If Lombard Street were on a sudden thrown into liquidation, and made to pay as much as it could on the spot, that 2,000,000 L. would be all which the Bank of England could pay to the depositing banks, and consequently all, besides the small cash in the till, which those banks could on a sudden pay to the persons who have deposited with them.

We see then that the banking reserve of the Bank of England--some 10,000,000 L. on an average of years now, and formerly much less--is all which is held against the liabilities of Lombard Street; and if that were all, we might well be amazed at the immense development of our credit systemin plain English. at the immense amount of our debts payable on demand, and the smallness of the sum of actual money which we keep to pay them if demanded. But there is more to come. Lombard Street is not only a place requiring to keep a reserve, it is itself a place where reserves are kept. All country bankers keep their reserve in London. They only retain in each country town the minimum of cash necessary to the transaction of the current business of that country town. Long experience has told them to a nicety how much this is, and they do not waste capital and lose profit by keeping more idle. They send the money to London, invest a part of it in securities, and keep the rest with the London bankers and the bill brokers. The habit of Scotch and Irish bankers is much the same. All their spare money is in London, and is invested as all other London money now is; and, therefore, the reserve in the Banking Department of the Bank of England is the banking reserve not only of the Bank of England, but of all Londonand not only of all London, but of all England, Ireland, and Scotland too.

Of late there has been a still further increase in our liabilities. Since the Franco-German war, we may be said to keep the European reserve also. Deposit Banking is indeed so small on the Continent, that no large reserve need be held on account of it. A reserve of the same sort which is needed in England and Scotland is not needed abroad. But all great communities have at times to pay large sums in cash, and of that cash a great store must be kept somewhere. Formerly there were two such stores in Europe, one was the Bank of France, and the other the Bank of England. But since the suspension of specie payments by the Bank of France, its use as a reservoir of specie is at an end. No one can draw a cheque on it and be sure of getting gold or silver for that cheque. Accordingly the whole liability for such international payments in cash is thrown on the Bank of England. No doubt foreigners cannot take from us our own money; they must send here 'value in some shape or other for all they take away. But they need not send 'cash;' they may send good bills and discount them in Lombard Street and take away any part of the produce, or all the produce, in bullion. It is only putting the same point in other words to say that all exchange operations are centering more and more in London. Formerly for many purposes Paris was a European settling-house, but now it has ceased to be so. The note of the Bank of France has not indeed been depreciated enough to disorder ordinary transactions. But any depreciation, however small--even the liability to depreciation without its reality--is enough to disorder exchange transactions. They are calculated to such an extremity of fineness that the change of a decimal may be fatal, and may turn a profit into a loss. Accordingly London has become the sole great settling-house of exchange transactions in Europe, instead of being formerly one of two. And this pre-eminence London will probably maintain, for it is a natural pre-eminence. The number of mercantile bills drawn upon London incalculably surpasses those drawn on any other European city; London is the place which receives more than any other place, and pays more than any other place, and therefore it is the natural 'clearing house.' The pre-eminence of Paris partly arose from a distribution of political power, which is already disturbed; but that of London depends on the regular course of commerce, which is singularly stable and hard to change.

Now that London is the clearing-house to foreign countries, London has a new liability to foreign countries. At whatever place many people have to make payments, at that place those people must keep money. A large deposit of foreign money in London is now necessary for the business of the world. During the immense payments from France to Germany, the sum in transituthe sum in London has perhaps been unusually large. But it will ordinarily be very great. The present political circumstances no doubt will soon change. We shall soon hold in Lombard Street far less of the money of foreign governments; but we shall hold more and more of the money of private persons; for the deposit at a clearing-house necessary to settle the balance of commerce must tend to increase as that commerce itself increases.

And this foreign deposit is evidently of a delicate and peculiar nature. It depends on the good opinion of foreigners, and that opinion may diminish or may change into a bad opinion. After the panic of 1866, especially after the suspension of Peel's Act (which many foreigners confound with a suspension of cash payments), a large amount of foreign money was withdrawn from London. And we may reasonably presume that in proportion as we augment the deposits of cash by foreigners in London, we augment both the chances and the disasters of a 'run' upon England.

And if that run should happen, the bullion to meet it must be taken from the Bank. There is no other large store in the country. The great exchange dealers may have a little for their own purposes, but they have no store worth mentioning in comparison with this. If a foreign creditor is so kind as to wait his time and buy the bullion as it comes into the country, he may be paid without troubling the Bank or distressing the money market. The German Government has recently been so kind; it was in no respect afraid. But a creditor who takes fright will not wait, and if he wants bullion in a hurry he must come to the Bank of England.

In consequence all our credit system depends on the Bank of England for its security. On the wisdom of the directors of that one Joint Stock Company, it depends whether England shall be solvent or insolvent. This may seem too strong, but it is not. All banks depend on the Bank of England, and all merchants depend on some banker. If a merchant have 10,000 L. at his bankers, and wants to pay it to some one in Germany, he will not be able to pay it unless his banker can pay him, and the banker will not be able to pay if the Bank of England should be in difficulties and cannot produce his 'reserve.'

The directors of the Bank are, therefore, in fact, if not in name, trustees for the public, to keep a banking reserve on their behalf; and it would naturally be expected either that they distinctly recognized this duty and engaged to perform it, or that their own self-interest was so strong in the matter that no engagement was needed. But so far from there being a distinct undertaking on the part of the Bank directors to perform this duty, many of them would scarcely acknowledge it, and some altogether deny it. Mr. Hankey, one of the most careful and most experienced of them, says in his book on the Bank of England, the best account of the practice and working of the Bank which anywhere exists--'I do not intend here to enter at any length on the subject of the general management of the Bank, meaning the Banking Department, as the principle upon which the business is conducted does not differ, as far as I am aware, from that of any wellconducted bank in London.' But, as anyone can see by the published figures, the Banking Department of the Bank of England keeps as a great reserve in bank notes and coin between 30 and 50 per cent of its liabilities, and the other banks only keep in bank notes and coin the bare minimum they need to open shop with. And such a constant difference indicates, I conceive, that the two are not managed on the same principle.

The practice of the Bank has, as we all know, been much and greatly improved. They do not now manage like the other Banks in Lombard Street. They keep an altogether different kind and quantity of reserve; but though the practice is mended the theory is not. There has never been a distinct resolution passed by the Directors of the Bank of England, and communicated by them to the public, stating even in the most general manner, how much reserve they mean to keep or how much they do not mean, or by what principle in this important matter they will be guided.

The position of the Bank directors is indeed most singular. On the one side a great city opinion--a great national opinion, I may say, for the nation has learnt much from many panics--requires the directors to keep a large reserve. The newspapers, on behalf of the nation, are always warning the directors to keep it, and watching that they do keep it; but, on the other hand, another less visible but equally constant pressure pushes the directors in exactly the reverse way, and inclines them to diminish the reserve.

This is the natural desire of all directors to make a good dividend for their shareholders. The more money lying idle the less, caeteris paribus, is the dividend; the less money lying idle the greater is the dividend. And at almost every meeting of the proprietors of the Bank of England, there is a conversation on this subject. Some proprietor says that he does not see why so much money is kept idle, and hints that the dividend ought to be more.

Indeed, it cannot be wondered at that the Bank proprietors do not quite like their position. Theirs is the oldest bank in the City, but their profits do not increase, while those of other banks most rapidly increase. In 1844, the dividend on the stock of the Bank of England was 7 per cent, and the price of the stock itself 212; the dividend now is 9 per cent, and the price of the stock 232. But in the same time the shares of the London and Westminster Bank, in spite of an addition of 100 per cent to the capital, have risen from 27 to 66, and the dividend from 6 per cent to 20 per cent. That the Bank proprietors should not like to see other companies getting richer than their company is only natural.

Some part of the lowness of the Bank dividend, and of the consequent small value of Bank stock, is undoubtedly caused by the magnitude of the Bank capital; but much of it is also due to the great amount of unproductive cashof cash which yields no interestthat the Banking Department of the Bank of England keeps lying idle. If we compare the London and Westminster Bankwhich is the first of the joint-stock banks in the public estimation and known to be very cautiously and carefully managedwith the Bank of England, we shall see the difference at once. The London and Westminster has only 13 per cent of its liabilities lying idle. The Banking Department of the Bank of England has over 40 per cent. So great a difference in the management must cause, and does cause, a great difference in the profits. Inevitably the shareholders of the Bank of England will dislike this great difference; more or less, they will always urge their directors to diminish (as far as possible) the unproductive reserve, and to augment as fall as possible their own dividend.

In most banks there would be a wholesome dread restraining the desire of the shareholders to reduce the reserve; they would fear to impair the credit of the bank. But fortunately or unfortunately, no one has any fear about the Bank of England. The English world at least believes that it will not, almost that it cannot, fail. Three times since 1844 the Banking Department has received assistance, and would have failed without it. In 1825, the entire concern almost suspended payment; in 1797, it actually did so. But still there is a faith in the Bank, contrary to experience, and despising evidence. No doubt in every one of these years the condition of the Bank, divided or undivided, was in a certain sense most sound; it could ultimately have paid all its creditors all it owed, and returned to its shareholders all their own capital. But ultimate payment is not what the creditors of a bank want; they want present, not postponed, payment; they want to be repaid according to agreement; the contract was that they should be paid on demand, and if they are not paid on demand they may be ruined. And that instant payment, in the years I speak of, the Bank of England certainly could not have made. But no one in London ever dreams of questioning the credit of the Bank, and the Bank never dreams that its own credit is in danger. Somehow everybody feels the Bank is sure to come right. In 1797, when it had scarcely any money left, the Government said not only that it need not pay away what remained, but that it must not. The 'effect of letters of licence' to break Peel's Act has confirmed the popular conviction that the Government is close behind the Bank, and will help it when wanted. Neither the Bank nor the Banking Department have ever had an idea of being put 'into liquidation;' most men would think as soon of 'winding up' the English nation.

Since then the Bank of England, as a bank, is exempted from the perpetual apprehension that makes other bankers keep a large reserve the apprehension of discreditit would seem particularly necessary that its managers should be themselves specially interested in keeping that reserve, and specially competent to keep it. But I need not say that the Bank directors have not their personal fortune at stake in the management of the Bank. They are rich City merchants, and their stake in the Bank is trifling in comparison with the rest of their wealth. If the

Bank were wound up, most of them would hardly in their income feel the difference. And what is more, the Bank directors are not trained bankers; they were not bred to the trade, and do not in general give the main power of their minds to it. They are merchants, most of whose time and most of whose real mind are occupied in making money in their own business and for themselves.

It might be expected that as this great public duty was cast upon the Banking Department of the Bank, the principal statesmen (if not Parliament itself) would have enjoined on them to perform it. But no distinct resolution of Parliament has ever enjoined it; scarcely any stray word of any influential statesman. And, on the contrary, there is a whole *catena* of authorities, beginning with Sir Robert Peel and ending with Mr. Lowe, which say that the Banking Department of the Bank of England is only a Bank like any other banka Company like other companies; that in this capacity it has no peculiar position, and no public duties at all. Nine-tenths of English statesmen, if they were asked as to the management of the Banking Department of the Bank of England, would reply that it was no business of theirs or of Parliament at all; that the Banking Department alone must look to it.

The result is that we have placed the exclusive custody of our entire banking reserve in the hands of a single board of directors not particularly trained for the duty--who might be called 'amateurs,' who have no particular interest above other people in keeping it undiminished--who acknowledge no obligation to keep it undiminished who have never been told by any great statesman or public authority that they are so to keep it or that they have anything to do with it who are named by and are agents for a proprietary which would have a greater income if it was diminished, who do not fear, and who need not fear, ruin, even if it were all gone and wasted.

That such an arrangement is strange must be plain; but its strangeness can only be comprehended when we know what the custody of a national banking reserve means, and how delicate and difficult it is.

II.

Such a reserve as we have seen is kept to meet sudden and unexpected demands. If the bankers of a country are asked for much more than is commonly wanted, then this reserve must be resorted to. What then are these extra demands? and how is this extra reserve to be used? Speaking broadly, these extra demands are of two kind--sone from abroad to meet foreign payments requisite to pay large and unusual foreign debts, and the other from at home to meet sudden apprehension or panic arising in any manner, rational or irrational.

No country has ever been so exposed as England to a foreign demand on its banking reserve, not only because at present England is a large borrower from foreign nations, but also (and much more) because no nation has ever had a foreign trade of such magnitude, in such varied objects, or so ramified through the world. The ordinary foreign trade of a country requires no cash; the exports on one side balance the imports on the other. But a sudden trade of import like the import of foreign corn after a bad harvestor (what is much less common, though there are cases of it) the cessation of any great export, causes a balance to become due, which must be paid in cash.

Now, the only source from which large sums of cash can be withdrawn in countries where banking is at all developed, is a 'bank reserve.' In England especially, except a few sums of no very considerable amount held by bullion dealers in the course of their business, there are no sums worth mentioning in cash out of the banks; an ordinary person could hardly pay a serious sum without going to some bank, even if he spent a month in trying. All persons who wish to pay a large sum in cash trench of necessity on the banking reserve. But then what is 'cash?' Within a country the action of a Government can settle the quantity, and therefore the value, of its currency; but outside its own country, no Government can do so. Bullion is the cash' of international trade; paper currencies are of no use there, and coins pass only as they contain more or less bullion.

When then the legal tender of a country is purely metallic, all that is necessary is that banks should keep a sufficient store of that 'legal tender.' But when the 'legal tender' is partly metal and partly paper, it is necessary that the paper 'legal tender'--the bank note--should be convertible into bullion. And here I should pass my limits, and enter on the theory of Peel's Act if I began to discuss the conditions of convertibility. I deal only with the primary pre-requisite of effectual foreign payments--a sufficient supply of the local legal tender; with the afterstep--the change of the local legal tender into the universally acceptable commodity cannot deal.

What I have to deal with is, for the present, ample enough. The Bank of England must keep a reserve of 'legal tender' to be used for foreign payments if itself fit, and to be used in obtaining bullion if itself unfit. And foreign payments are sometimes very large, and often very sudden. The 'cotton drain,' as it is called--the drain to the East to pay for Indian cotton during the American Civil War took many millions from this country for a series of years. A bad harvest must take millions in a single year. In order to find such great sums, the Bank of England requires the steady use of an effectual instrument.

That instrument is the elevation of the rate of interest. If the interest of money be raised, it is proved by experience that money does come to Lombard Street, and theory shows that it ought to come. To fully explain the matter I must go deep into the theory of the exchanges, but the general notion is plain enough. Loanable capital, like every other commodity, comes where there is most to be made of it. Continental bankers and others instantly send great sums here, as soon as the rate of interest shows that it can be done profitably. While English credit is good, a rise of the value of money in Lombard Street immediately by a banking operation brings money to Lombard Street. And there is also a slower mercantile operation. The rise in the rate of discount acts immediately on the trade of this country. Prices fall here; in consequence imports are diminished, exports are increased, and, therefore, there is more likelihood of a balance in bullion coming to this country after the rise in the rate than there was before.

Whatever personsone bank or many banksin any country hold the banking reserve of that country, ought at the very beginning of an unfavourable foreign exchange at once to raise the rate of interest, so as to prevent their reserve from being diminished farther, and so as to replenish it by imports of bullion.

This duty, up to about the year 1860, the Bank of England did not perform at all, as I shall show farther on. A more miserable history can hardly be found than that of the attempts of the Bankif indeed they can be called attempts--to keep a reserve and to manage a foreign drain between the year 1819 (when cash payments were resumed by the Bank, and when our modern Money Market may be said to begin) and the year 1857. The panic of that year for the first time taught the Bank directors wisdom, and converted them to sound principles. The present policy of the Bank is an infinite improvement on the policy before 1857: the two must not be for an instant confounded; but nevertheless, as I shall hereafter show, the present policy is now still most defective, and much discussion and much effort. will be wanted before that policy becomes what it ought to be.

A domestic drain is very different. Such a drain arises from a disturbance of credit within the country, and the difficulty of dealing with it is the greater, because it is often caused, or at least often enhanced, by a foreign drain. Times without number the public have been alarmed mainly because they saw that the Banking reserve was already low, and that it was daily getting lower. The two maladiesan external drain and an internal-often attack the money market at once. What then ought to be done?

In opposition to what might be at first sight supposed, the best way for the bank or banks who have the custody of the bank reserve to deal with a drain arising from internal discredit, is to lend freely. The first instinct of everyone is the contrary. There being a large demand on a fund which you want to preserve, the most obvious way to preserve it is to hoard it--to get in as much as you can, and to let nothing go out which you can help. But every banker knows that this is not the way to diminish discredit. This discredit means, 'an opinion that you have not got any money,' and to dissipate that opinion, you must, if possible, show that you have money: you must employ it for the public benefit in order that the public may know that you have it. The time for economy and for accumulation is before. A good banker will have accumulated in ordinary times the reserve he is to make use of in extraordinary times.

Ordinarily discredit does not at first settle on any particular bank, still less does it at first concentrate itself on the bank or banks holding the principal cash reserve. These banks are almost sure to be those in best credit, or they would not be in that position, and, having the reserve, they are likely to look stronger and seem stronger than any others. At first, incipient panic amounts to a kind of vague conversation: Is A. B. as good as he used to be? Has not C. D. lost money? and a thousand such questions. A hundred people are talked about, and a thousand think,--'Am I talked about, or am I not?' 'Is my credit as good as it used to be, or is it less?' And every day, as a panic grows, this floating suspicion becomes both more intense and more diffused; it attacks more persons; and attacks them all more virulently than at first. All men of experience, therefore, try to strengthen themselves,' as it is called, in the early stage of a panic; they borrow money while they can; they come to their banker and offer bills for discount, which commonly they would not have offered for days or weeks to come. And if the merchant be a regular customer, a banker does not like to refuse, because if he does he will be said, or may be said, to be in want of money, and so may attract the panic to himself. Not only merchants but all persons under pecuniary liabilities--present or imminent--feel this wish to 'strengthen themselves,' and in proportion to those liabilities. Especially is this the case with what may be called the auxiliary dealers in credit. Under any system of banking there will always group themselves about the main bank or banks (in which is kept the reserve) a crowd of smaller money dealers, who watch the minutae of bills, look into special securities which busy bankers have not time for, and so gain a livelihood. As business grows, the number of such subsidiary persons augments. The various modes in which money may be lent have each their peculiarities, and persons who devote themselves to one only lend in that way more safely, and therefore more cheaply. In time of panic, these subordinate dealers in money will always come to the principal dealers. In ordinary times, the intercourse between the two is probably close enough. The little dealer is probably in the habit of pledging his 'securities' to the larger dealer at a rate less than he has himself charged, and of running into the market to lend again. His time and brains are his principal capital, and he wants to be always using them. But in times of incipient panic, the minor money dealer always becomes alarmed. His credit is never very established or very wide; he always fears that he may be the person on whom current suspicion will fasten, and often he is so. Accordingly he asks the larged dealer for advances. A number of such persons ask all the large dealers--those who have the money--the holders of the reserve. And then the plain problem before the great dealers comes to be 'How shall we best protect ourselves? No doubt the immediate advance to these second-class dealers is annoying, but may not the refusal of it even be dangerous? A panic grows by what it feeds on; if it devours these second-class men, shall we, the first class, be safe?'

A panic, in a word, is a species of neuralgia, and according to the rules of science you must not starve it. The holders of the cash reserve must be ready not only to keep it for their own liabilities, but to advance it most freely for the liabilities of others. They must lend to merchants, to minor bankers, to 'this man and that man,' whenever the security is good. In wild periods of alarm, one failure makes many, and the best way to prevent the derivative failures is to arrest the primary failure which causes them. The way in which the panic of 1825 was stopped by advancing money has been described in so broad and graphic a way that the passage has become classical. 'We lent it,' said Mr. Harman, on behalf of the Bank of England, 'by every possible means and in modes we had never adopted before; we took in stock on security, we purchased Exchequer bills, we made advances on Exchequer bills, we not only discounted outright, but we made advances on the deposit of bills of exchange to an immense amount, in short, by every possible means consistent with the safety of the Bank, and we were not on some occasions over-nice. Seeing the dreadful state in which the public were, we rendered every assistance in our power.' After a day or two of this treatment, the entire panic subsided, and the 'City' was quite calm.

The problem of managing a panic must not be thought of as mainly a 'banking' problem. It is primarily a mercantile one. All merchants are under liabilities; they have bills to meet soon, and they can only pay those bills by discounting bills on other merchants. In other words, all merchants are dependent on borrowing money, and large merchants are dependent on borrowing much money. At the slightest symptom of panic many merchants want to borrow more than usual; they think they will supply themselves with the means of meeting their bills while those means are still forthcoming. If the bankers gratify the merchants, they must lend largely just when they like it least; if they do not gratify them, there is a panic.

On the surface there seems a great inconsistency in all this. First, you establish in some bank or banks a certain reserve; you make of it or them a kind of ultimate treasury, where the last shilling of the country is deposited and kept. And then you go on to say that this final treasury is also to be the last lending-house; that out of it unbounded, or at any rate immense, advances are to be made when no once else lends. This seems like saying--first, that the reserve should be kept, and then that it should not be kept. But there is no puzzle in the matter. The ultimate banking reserve of a country (by whomsoever kept) is not kept out of show, but for certain essential purposes, and one of those purposes is the meeting a demand for cash caused by an alarm within the country. It is not unreasonable that our ultimate treasure in particular cases should be lent; on the contrary, we keep that treasure for the very reason that in particular cases it should be lent.

When reduced to abstract principle, the subject comes to this. An 'alarm' is an opinion that the money of certain persons will not pay their creditors when those creditors want to be paid. If possible, that alarm is best met by enabling those persons to pay their creditors to the very moment. For this purpose only a little money is wanted. If that alarm is not so met, it aggravates into a panic, which is an opinion that most people, or very many people, will not pay their creditors; and this too can only be met by enabling all those persons to pay what they owe, which takes a great deal of money. No one has enough money, or anything like enough, but the holders of the bank reserve.

Not that the help so given by the banks holding that reserve necessarily diminishes it. Very commonly the panic extends as far, or almost as far, as the bank or banks which hold the reserve, but does not touch it or them at all. In this case it is enough if the dominant bank or banks, so to speak, pledge their credit for those who want it. Under our present system it is often quite enough that a merchant or a banker gets the advance made to him put to his credit in the books of the Bank of England; he may never draw a cheque on it, or, if he does, that cheque may come in again to the credit of some other customer, who lets it remain on his account. An increase of loans at such times is often an increase of the liabilities of the bank, not a diminution of its reserve. Just so before 1844, an issue of notes, as in to quell a panic entirely internal did not diminish the bullion reserve. The notes went out, but they did not return. They were issued as loans to the public, but the public wanted no more; they never presented them for payment; they never asked that sovereigns should be given for them. But the acceptance of a great liability during an augmenting alarm, though not as bad as an equal advance of cash, is the thing next worst. At any moment the cash may be demanded. Supposing the panic to grow, it will be demanded, and the reserve will be lessened accordingly.

No doubt all precautions may, in the end, be unavailing. 'On extraordinary occasions,' says Ricardo, 'a general panic may seize the country, when every one becomes desirous of possessing himself of the precious metals as the most convenient mode of realising or concealing his property, against such panic banks have no security *on any system.*' The bank or banks which hold the reserve may last a little longer than the others; but if apprehension pass a certain bound, they must perish too. The use of credit is, that it enables debtors to use a certain part of the money their creditors have lent them. If all those creditors demand all that money at once, they cannot have it, for that which their debtors have used, is for the time employed, and not to be obtained. With the advantages of credit we must take the disadvantages too; but to lessen them as much as we can, we must keep a great store of ready money always available, and advance out of it very freely in periods of panic, and in times of incipient alarm.

The management of the Money Market is the more difficult, because, as has been said, periods of internal panic and external demand for bullion commonly occur together. The foreign drain empties the Bank till, and that emptiness, and the resulting rise in the rate of discount, tend to frighten the market. The holders of the reserve have, therefore, to treat two opposite maladies at once--one requiring stringent remedies, and especially a rapid rise in the rate of interest; and the other, an alleviative treatment with large and ready loans.

Before we had much specific experience, it was not easy to prescribe for this compound disease; but now we know how to deal with it. We must look first to the foreign drain, and raise the rate of interest as high as may be necessary. Unless you can stop the foreign export, you cannot allay the domestic alarm. The Bank will get poorer and poorer, and its poverty will protract or renew the apprehension. And at the rate of interest so raised, the holdersone or more-of the final Bank reserve must lend freely. Very large loans at very high rates are the best remedy for the worst malady of the money market when a foreign drain is added to a domestic drain. Any notion that money is not to be had, or that it may not be had at any price, only raises alarm to panic and enhances panic to madness. But though the rule is clear, the greatest delicacy, the finest and best skilled judgment, are needed to deal at once with such great and contrary evils.

And great as is the delicacy of such a problem in all countries, it is far greater in England now than it was or is elsewhere. The strain thrown by a panic on the final bank reserve is proportional to the magnitude of a country's commerce, and to the number and size of the dependent banks--banks, that is, holding no cash reservethat are grouped around the central bank or banks. And in both respects our system causes a stupendous strain. The magnitude of our commerce, and the number and magnitude of the banks which depend on the Bank of England, are undeniable. There are very many more persons under great liabilities than there are, or ever were, anywhere else. At the commencement of every panic, all persons under such liabilities try to supply themselves with the means of meeting those liabilities while they can. This causes a great demand for new loans. And so far from being able to meet it, the bankers who do not keep an extra reserve at that time borrow largely, or do not renew large loansvery likely do both.

London bankers, other than the Bank of England, effect this in several ways. First, they have probably discounted bills to a large amount for the bill brokers, and if these bills are paid, they decline discounting any others to replace them. The directors of the London and Westminster Bank had, in the panic of 1857, discounted millions of such bills, and they justly said that if those bills were paid they would have an amount of cash far more than sufficient for any demand. But how were those bills to be paid? Some one else must lend the money to pay them. The mercantile community could not on a sudden bear to lose so large a sum of borrowed money; they have been used to rely on it, and they could not carry on their business without it. Least of all could they bear it at the beginning of a panic, when everybody wants more money than usual. Speaking broadly, those bills can only be paid by the discount of other bills. When the bills (suppose) of a Manchester warehouseman which he gave to the manufacturer become due, he cannot, as a rule, pay for them at once in cash; he has bought on credit, and he has sold on credit. He is but a middleman. To pay his own bill to the maker of the goods, he must discount the bills he has received from the shopkeepers to whom he has sold the goods; but if there is a sudden cessation in the means of discount, he will not be able to discount them. All our mercantile community must obtain new loans to pay old debts. If some one else did not pour into the market the money which the banks like the London and Westminster Bank take out of it, the bills held by the London and Westminster Bank could not be paid.

Who then is to pour in the new money? Certainly not the bill brokers. They have been used to re-discount with such banks as the London and Westminster millions of bills, and if they see that they are not likely to be able to re-discount those bills, they instantly protect themselves and do not discount them. Their business does not allow them to keep much cash unemployed. They give interest for all the money deposited with the--man interest often nearly approaching the interest they can charge; as they can only keep a small reserve a panic tells on them more quickly than on anyone else. They stop their discounts, or much diminish their discounts, immediately. There is no new money to be had from them, and the only place at which they can have it is the Bank of England.

There is even a simpler case: the banker who is uncertain of his credit, and wants to increase his cash, may have money on deposit at the bill brokers. If he wants to replenish his reserve, he may ask for it, suppose, just when the alarm is beginning. But if a great number of persons do this very suddenly, the bill brokers will not at once be able to pay without borrowing. They have excellent bills in their case, but these will not be due for some days; and the demand from the more or less alarmed bankers is for payment at once and to-day. Accordingly the bill broker takes refuge at the Bank of England the only place where at such a moment new money is to be had.

The case is just the same if the banker wants to sell Consols, or to call in money lent on Consols. These he reckons as part of his reserve. And in ordinary times nothing can be better. According to the saying, you 'can sell Consols on a Sunday.' In a time of no alarm, or in any alarm affecting that particular banker only, he can rely on such reserve without misgiving. But not so in a general panic. Then, if he wants to sell 500,000 L. worth of Consols, he will not find 500,000 L. of fresh money ready to come into the market. All ordinary bankers are wanting to sell, or thinking they may have to sell. The only resource is the Bank of England. In a great panic, Consols cannot be sold unless the Bank of

England will advance to the buyer, and no buyer can obtain advances on Consols at such a time unless the Bank of England will lend to him.

The case is worse if the alarm is not confined to the great towns, but is diffused through the country. As a rule, country bankers only keep so much barren cash as is necessary for their common business. All the rest they leave at the bill brokers, or at the interest-giving banks, or invest in Consols and such securities. But in a panic they come to London and want this money. And it is only from the Bank of England that they can get it, for all the rest of London want their money for themselves.

If we remember that the liabilities of Lombard Street payable on demand are far larger than those of any like market, and that the liabilities of the country are greater still, we can conceive the magnitude of the pressure on the Bank of England when both Lombard Street and the country suddenly and at once come upon it for aid. No other bank was ever exposed to a demand so formidable, for none ever before kept the banking reserve for such a nation as the English. The mode in which the Bank of England meets this great responsibility is very curious. It unquestionably does make enormous advances in every panic

In 1847 the loans on 'private securities'
increased from   18,963,000 L to 20,409,000 L
1857 ditto ditto   20,404,000 L to 31,350,000 L
1866 ditto ditto   18,507,000 L to 33,447,000 L

But, on the other hand, as we have seen, though the Bank, more or less, does its duty, it does not distinctly acknowledge that it is its duty. We are apt to be solemnly told that the Banking Department of the Bank of England is only a bank like other banks--that it has no peculiar duty in times of panic--that it then is to look to itself alone, as other banks look. And there is this excuse for the Bank. Hitherto questions of banking have been so little discussed in comparison with questions of currency, that the duty of the Bank in time of panic has been put on a wrong ground.

It is imagined that because bank notes are a legal tender, the Bank has some peculiar duty to help other people. But bank notes are only a legal tender at the Issue Department, not at the Banking Department, and the accidental combination of the two departments in the same building gives the Banking Department no aid in meeting a panic. If the Issue Department were at Somerset House, and if it issued Government notes there, the position of the Banking Department under the present law would be exactly what it is now. No doubt, formerly the Bank of England could issue what it pleased, but that historical reminiscence makes it no stronger now that it can no longer so issue. We must deal with what is, not with what was.

And a still worse argument is also used. It is said that because the Bank of England keeps the 'State account' and is the Government banker, it is a sort of 'public institution' and ought to help everybody. But the custody of the taxes which have been collected and which wait to be expended is a duty quite apart from panics. The Government money may chance to be much or little when the panic comes. There is no relation or connection between the two. And the State, in getting the Bank to keep what money it may chance to have, or in borrowing of it what money it may chance to want, does not hire it to stop a panic or much help it if it tries.

The real reason has not been distinctly seen. As has been already said--but on account of its importance and perhaps its novelty it is worth saying againwhatever bank or banks keep the ultimate banking reserve of the country must lend that reserve most freely in time of apprehension, for that is one of the characteristic uses of the bank reserve, and the mode in which it attains one of the main ends for which it is kept. Whether rightly or wrongly, at present and in fact the Bank of England keeps our ultimate bank reserve, and therefore it must use it in this manner.

And though the Bank of England certainly do make great advances in time of panic, yet as they do not do so on any distinct principle, they naturally do it hesitatingly, reluctantly, and with misgiving. In 1847, even in 1866--the latest panic, and the one in which on the whole the Bank acted the best--there was nevertheless an instant when it was believed the Bank would not advance on Consols, or at least hesitated to advance on them. The moment this was reported in the City and telegraphed to the country, it made the panic indefinitely worse. In fact, to make large advances in this faltering way is to incur the evil of making them without obtaining the advantage. What is wanted and what is necessary to stop a panic is to diffuse the impression, that though money may be dear, still money is to be had. If people could be really convinced that they could have money if they wait a day or two, and that utter ruin is not coming, most likely they would cease to run in such a mad way for money. Either shut the Bank at once, and say it will not lend more than it commonly lends, or lend freely, boldly, and so that the public may feel you mean to go on lending. To lend a great deal, and yet not give the public confidence that you will lend sufficiently and effectually, is the worst of all policies; but it is the policy now pursued.

In truth, the Bank do not lend from the motives which should make a bank lend. The holders of the Bank reserve ought to lend at once and most freely in an incipient panic, because they fear destruction in the panic. They ought not to do it to serve others; they ought to do it to serve themselves. They ought to know that this bold policy is the only safe one, and for that reason they ought to choose it. But the Bank directors are not afraid. Even at the last moment they say that 'whatever happens to the community, they can preserve themselves.' Both in 1847 and 1857 (I believe also in 1866, though there is no printed evidence of it) the Bank directors contended that the Banking Department was quite safe though its reserve was nearly all gone, and that it could strengthen itself by selling securities and by refusing to discount. But this is a complete dream. The Bank of England could not sell 'securities,' for in an extreme panic there is no one else to buy securities. The Bank cannot stay still and wait till its bills are paid, and so fill its coffers, for unless it discounts equivalent bills, the bills which it has already discounted will not be paid. 'When the reserve in the ultimate bank or banks--those keeping the reserveruns low, it cannot be augmented by the same means that other and dependent banks commonly adopt to maintain their reserve, for the dependent banks trust that at such moments the ultimate banks will be discounting more than usual and lending more than usual. But ultimate banks have no similar rear-guard to rely upon.

I shall have failed in my purpose if I have not proved that the system of entrusting all our reserve to a single board, like that of the Bank directors, is very anomalous; that it is very dangerous; that its bad consequences, though much felt, have not been fully seen; that they have been obscured by traditional arguments and hidden in the dust of ancient controversies.

But it will be said--What would be better? What other system could there be? We are so accustomed to a system of banking, dependent for its cardinal function on a single bank, that we can hardly conceive of any other. But the natural system--that which would have sprung up if Government had let banking alone--is that of many banks of equal or not altogether unequal size. In all other trades competition brings the traders to a rough approximate equality. In cotton spinning, no single firm far and permanently outstrips the others. There is no tendency to a monarchy in the cotton world; nor, where banking has been left free, is there any tendency to a monarchy in banking either. In Manchester, in Liverpool, and all through England, we have a great number of banks, each with a business more or less good, but we have no single bank with any sort of predominance; nor is there any such bank in Scotland. In the new world of Joint Stock Banks outside the Bank of England, we see much the same phenomenon. One or more get for a time a better business than the others, but no single bank permanently obtains an unquestioned predominance. None of them gets so much before the others that the others voluntarily place their reserves in its keeping. A republic with many competitors of a size or sizes suitable to the business, is the constitution of every trade if left to itself, and of banking as much as any other. A monarchy in any trade is a sign of some anomalous advantage, and of some intervention from without.

I shall be at once asked--Do you propose a revolution? Do you propose to abandon the one-reserve system, and create anew a many-reserve system? My plain answer is that I do not propose it. I know it would be childish. Credit in business is like loyalty in Government. You must take what you can find of it, and work with it if possible. A theorist may easily map out a scheme of Government in which Queen Victoria could be dispensed with. He may make a theory that, since we admit and we know that the House of Commons is the real sovereign, any other sovereign is superfluous; but for practical purposes, it is not even worth while to examine these arguments. Queen Victoria is loyally obeyed--without doubt, and without reasoning--by millions of human beings. If those millions began to argue, it would not be easy to persuade them to obey Queen Victoria, or anything else. Effectual arguments to convince the people who need convincing are wanting. Just so, an immense system of credit, founded on the Bank of England as its pivot and its basis, now exists. The English people, and foreigners too, trust it implicitly. Every banker knows that if he has to prove that he is worthy of credit, however good may be his arguments, in fact his credit is gone: but what we have requires no proof. The whole rests on an instinctive confidence generated by use and years. Nothing would persuade the English people to abolish the Bank of England; and if some calamity swept it away, generations must elapse before at all the same trust would be placed in any other equivalent. A many-reserve system, if some miracle should put it down in Lombard Street, would seem monstrous there. Nobody would understand it, or confide in it. Credit is a power which may grow, but cannot be constructed. Those who live under a great and firm system of credit must consider that if they break up that one they will never see another, for it will take years upon years to make a successor to it.

On this account, I do not suggest that we should return to a natural or many-reserve system of banking. I should only incur useless ridicule if I did suggest it. Nor can I propose that we should adopt the simple and straightforward expedient by which the French have extricated themselves from the same difficulty. In France all banking rests on the Bank of France, even more than in England all rests on the Bank of England. The Bank of France keeps the final banking reserve, and it keeps the currency reserve too. But the State does not trust such a function to a board of merchants, named by shareholders. The nation itself--the Executive Government--names the governor and deputy-governor of the Bank of France. These officers have, indeed, beside them a council of 'regents,' or directors, named by the shareholders. But they need not attend to that council unless they think fit; they are appointed to watch over the national interest, and, in so doing, they may disregard the murmurs of the 'regents' if they like. And in theory, there is much to be said for this plan. The keeping the single banking reserve being a national function, it is at least plausible to argue that Government should choose the functionaries. No doubt such a political intervention is contrary to the sound economical doctrine that 'banking is a trade, and only a trade.' But Government forgot that doctrine when, by privileges and monopolies, it made a single bank predominant over all others, and established the one-reserve system. As that system exists, a logical Frenchman consistently enough argues that the State should watch and manage it. But no such plan would answer in England. We have not been trained to care for logical sequence in our institutions, or rather we have been trained not to care for it. And the practical result for which we do care would in this case be bad. The governor of the Bank would be a high Parliamentary official, perhaps in the Cabinet, and would change as chance majorities and the strength of parties decide. A trade peculiarly requiring consistency and special attainment would be managed by a shifting and untrained ruler. In fact, the whole plan would seem to an Englishman of business palpably absurd; he would not consider it, he would not think it worth considering. That it works fairly well in France, and that there are specious arguments of theory for it, would not be sufficient to his mind.

All such changes being out of the question, I can propose only three remedies.

First. There should be a clear understanding between the Bank and the public that, since the Bank hold out ultimate banking reserve, they will recognise and act on the obligations which this implies; that they will replenish it in times of foreign demand as fully, and Lend it in times of internal panic as freely and readily, as plain principles of banking require.

This looks very different from the French plan, but it is not so different in reality. In England we can often effect, by the indirect compulsion of opinion, what other countries must effect by the direct compulsion of Government. We can do so in this case. The Bank directors now fear public opinion exceedingly; probably no kind of persons are so sensitive to newspaper criticism. And this is very natural. Our statesmen, it is true, are much more blamed, but they have generally served a long apprenticeship to sharp criticism. If they still care for it (and some do after years of experience much more than the world thinks), they care less for it than at first, and have come to regard it as an unavoidable and incessant irritant, of which they shall never be rid. But a bank director undergoes no similar training and hardening. His functions at the Bank fill a very small part of his time; all the rest of his life (unless he be in Parliament) is spent in retired and mercantile industry. He is not subjected to keen and public criticism, and is not taught to bear it. Especially when once in his life he becomes, by rotation, governor, he is most anxious that the two years of office shall 'go off well.' He is apt to be irritated even by objections to principles on which he acts, and cannot bear with equanimity censure which is pointed and personal. At present I am not sure if this sensitiveness is beneficial. As the exact position of the Bank of England in the Money Market is indistinctly seen, there is no standard to which a Bank governor can appeal. He is always in fear that 'something may be said;' but not quite knowing on what side that 'something' may be, his fear is but an indifferent guide to him. But if the cardinal doctrine were accepted, if it were acknowledged that the Bank is charged with the custody of our sole banking reserve, and is bound to deal with it according to admitted principles, then a governor of the Bank could look to those principles. He would know which way criticism was coming. If he was guided by the code, he would have a plain defence. And then we may be sure that old men of business would not deviate from the code. At present the Board of Directors are a sort of semi-trustees for the nation. I would have them real trustees, and with a good trust deed.

Secondly. The government of the Bank should be improved in a manner to be explained. We should diminish the 'amateur' element; we should augment the trained banking element; and we should ensure more constancy in the administration.

Thirdly. As these two suggestions are designed to make the Bank as strong as possible, we should look at the rest of our banking system, and try to reduce the demands on the Bank as much as we can. The central machinery being inevitably frail, we should carefully and as much as possible diminish the strain upon it.

But to explain these proposals, and to gain a full understanding of many arguments that have been used, we must look more in detail at the component parts of Lombard street, and at the curious set of causes which have made it assume its present singular structure.

CHAPTER III.

How Lombard Street Came to Exist, and Why It Assumed Its Present Form.

In the last century, a favourite subject of literary ingenuity was 'conjectural history,' as it was then called. Upon grounds of probability a fictitious sketch was made of the possible origin of things existing. If this kind of speculation were now applied to banking, the natural and first idea would be that large systems of deposit banking grew up in the early world, just as they grow up now in any large English colony. As soon as any such community becomes rich enough to have much money, and compact enough to be able to lodge its money in single banks, it at once begins so to do. English colonists do not like the risk of keeping their money, and they wish to make an interest on it. They carry from home the idea and the habit of banking, and they take to it as soon as they can in their new world. Conjectural history would be inclined to say that all banking began thus: but such history is rarely of any value. The basis of it is false. It assumes that what works most easily when established is that which it would be the most easy to establish, and that what seems simplest when familiar would be most easily appreciated by the mind though unfamiliar. But exactly the contrary is true. Many things which seem simple and which work well when firmly established, are very hard to establish among new people, and not very easy to explain to them. Deposit banking is of this sort. Its essence is that a very large number of persons agree to trust a very few persons, or some one person. Banking would not be a profitable trade if bankers were not a small number, and depositors in comparison an immense number. But to get a great number of persons to do exactly the same thing is always very difficult, and nothing but a very palpable necessity will make them on a sudden begin to do it. And there is no such palpable necessity in banking. If you take a country town in France, even now, you will not find any such system of banking as ours. Cheque-books are unknown, and money kept on running account by bankers is rare. People store their money in a caisse at their houses. Steady savings, which are waiting for investment, and which are sure not to be soon wanted, may be lodged with bankers; but the common floating cash of the community is kept by the community themselves at home. They prefer to keep it so, and it would not answer a banker's purpose to make expensive arrangements for keeping it otherwise. If a 'branch,' such as the National Provincial Bank opens in an English country town, were opened in a corresponding French one, it would not pay its expenses. You could not get any sufficient number of Frenchmen to agree to put their money there. And so it is in all countries not of British descent, though in various degrees. Deposit banking is a very difficult thing to begin, because people do not like to let their money out of their sight, especially do not like to let it out of sight without securitystill more, cannot all at once agree on any single person to whom they are content to trust it unseen and unsecured. Hypothetical history, which explains the past by. what is simplest and commonest in the present, is in banking, as in most things, quite untrue.

The real history is very different. New wants are mostly supplied by adaptation, not by creation or foundation. Something having been created to satisfy an extreme want, it is used to satisfy less pressing wants, or to supply additional conveniences. On this account, political Government--the oldest institution in the worldhas been the hardest worked. At the beginning of history, we find it doing everything which society wants done, and forbidding everything which society does not wish done. In trade, at present, the first commerce in a new place is a general shop, which, beginning with articles of real necessity, comes shortly to supply the oddest accumulation of petty comforts. And the history of banking has been the same. The first banks were not founded for our system of deposit banking, or for anything like it. They were founded for much more pressing reasons, and having been founded, they, or copies from them, were applied to our modern uses.

The earliest banks of Italy, where the name began, were finance companies. The Bank of St. George, at Genoa, and other banks founded in imitation of it, were at first only companies to make loans to, and float loans for, the Governments of the cities in which they were formed. The want of money is an urgent want of Governments at most periods, and seldom more urgent than it was in the tumultuous Italian Republics of the Middle Ages. After these banks had been long established, they began to do what we call banking business; but at first they never thought of it. The great banks of the North of Europe had their origin in a want still more curious. The notion of its being a prime business of a bank to give good coin has passed out of men's memories; but wherever it is felt, there is no want of business more keen and urgent. Adam Smith describes it so admirably that it would be stupid not to quote his words:--'The currency of a great state, such as France or England, generally consists almost entirely of its own coin. Should this currency, therefore, be at any time worn, clipt, or otherwise degraded below its standard value, the state by a reformation of its coin can effectually re-establish its currency. But the currency of a small state, such as Genoa or Hamburgh, can seldom consist altogether in its own coin, but must be made up, in a great measure, of the coins of all the neighbouring states with which its inhabitants have a continual intercourse. Such a state, therefore, by reforming its coin, will not always be able to reform its currency. If foreign bills of exchange are paid in this currency, the uncertain value of any sum, of what is in its own nature so uncertain, must render the exchange always very much against such a state, its currency being, in all foreign states, necessarily valued even below what it is worth.

'In order to remedy the inconvenience to which this disadvantageous exchange must have subjected their merchants, such small states, when they began to attend to the interest of trade, have frequently enacted, that foreign bills of exchange of a certain value should be paid, not in common currency, but by an order upon, or by a transfer in, the books of a certain bank, established upon the credit, and under the protection of the state, this bank being always obliged to pay, in good and true money, exactly according to the standard of the state. The banks of Venice, Genoa, Amsterdam, Hamburgh and Nuremburg, seem to have been all originally established with this view, though some of them may have afterwards been made subservient to other purposes. The money of such banks, being better than the common currency of the country, necessarily bore an agio, which was greater or smaller, according as the currency was supposed to be more or less degraded below the standard of the state. The agio of the bank of Hamburgh, for example, which is said to be commonly about fourteen per cent, is the supposed difference between the good standard money of the state, and the clipt, worn, and diminished currency poured into it from all the neighbouring states.

'Before 1609 the great quantity of clipt and worn foreign coin, which the extensive trade of Amsterdam brought from all parts of Europe, reduced the value of its currency about 9 per cent below that of good money fresh from the mint. Such money no sooner appeared than it was melted down or carried away, as it always is in such circumstances. The merchants, with plenty of currency, could not always find a sufficient quantity of good money to pay their bills of exchange; and the value of those bills, in spite of several regulations which were made to prevent it, became in a great measure uncertain.

'In order to remedy these inconveniences, a bank was established in 1609 under the guarantee of the City. This bank received both foreign coin, and the light and worn coin of the country at its real intrinsic value in the good standard money of the country, deducting only so much as was necessary for defraying the expense of coinage, and the other necessary expense of management. For the value which remained, after this small deduction was made, it gave a credit in its books. This credit was called bank money, which, as it represented money exactly according to the standard of the mint, was always of the same real value, and intrinsically worth more than current money. It was at the same time enacted, that all bills drawn upon or negotiated at Amsterdam of the value of six hundred guilders and upwards should be paid in bank money, which at once took away all uncertainty in the value of those bills. Every merchant, in consequence of this regulation, was obliged to keep an account with the bank in order to pay his foreign bills of exchange, which necessarily occasioned a certain demand for bank money.'

Again, a most important function of early banks is one which the present banks retain, though it is subsidiary to their main use; viz. the function of remitting money. A man brings money to the bank to meet a payment which he desires to make at a great distance, and the bank, having a connection with other banks, sends it where it is wanted. As soon as bills of exchange are given upon a large scale, this remittance is a very pressing requirement. Such bills must be made payable at a place convenient to the seller of the goods in payment of which they are given, perhaps at the great town where his warehouse is. But this may be very far from the retail shop of the buyer who bought those goods to sell them again in the country. For these, and a multitude of purposes, the instant and regular remittance of money is an early necessity of growing trade; and that remittance it was a first object of early banks to accomplish.

These are all uses other than those of deposit banking which banks supplied that afterwards became in our English sense deposit banks. By supplying these uses, they gained the credit that afterwards enabled them to gain a living as deposit banks. Being trusted for one purpose, they came to be trusted for a purpose quite different, ultimately far more important, though at first less keenly pressing. But these wants only affect a few persons, and therefore bring the bank under the notice of a few only. The real introductory function which deposit banks at first perform is much more popular, and it is only when they can perform this more popular kind of business that deposit banking ever spreads quickly and extensively. This function is the supply of the paper circulation to the country, and it will be observed that I am not about to overstep my limits and discuss this as a question of currency. In what form the best paper currency can be supplied to a country is a question of economical theory with which I do not meddle here. I am only narrating unquestionable history, not dealing with an argument where every step is disputed. And part of this certain history is that the best way to diffuse banking in a community is to allow the banker to issue banknotes of small amount that can supersede the metal currency. This amounts to a subsidy to each banker to enable him to keep open a bank till depositors choose to come to it. The country where deposit banking is most diffused is Scotland, and there the original profits were entirely derived from the circulation. The note issue is now a most trifling part of the liabilities of the Scotch banks, but it was once their mainstay and source of profit. A curious book, lately published, has enabled us to follow the course of this in detail. The Bank of Dundee, now amalgamated with the Royal Bank of Scotland, was founded in 1763, and had become before its amalgamation, eight or nine years since, a bank of considerable deposits. But for twenty-five years from its foundation it had no deposits at all. It subsisted mostly on its note issue, and a little on its remittance business. Only in 1792, after nearly thirty years, it began to gain deposits, but from that time they augmented very rapidly. The banking history of England has been the same, though we have no country bank accounts in detail which go back so far. But probably up to 1830 in England, or thereabouts, the main profit of banks was derived from the circulation, and for many years after that the deposits were treated as very minor matters, and the whole of so-called banking discussion turned on questions of circulation. We are still living in the debris of that controversy, for, as I have so often said, people can hardly think of the structure of Lombard Street, except with reference to the paper currency and to the Act of 1844, which regulates it now. The French are still in the same epoch of the subject. The great enquete of 1865 is almost wholly taken up with currency matters, and mere banking is treated as subordinate. And the accounts of the Bank of France show why. The last weekly statement before the German war showed that the circulation of the Bank of France was as much as 59,244,000 L., and that the private deposits were only 17,127,000 L. Now the private deposits are about the same, and the circulation is 112,000,000 L. So difficult is it in even a great country like France for the deposit system of banking to take root, and establish itself with the strength and vigour that it has in England.

The experience of Germany is the same. The accounts preceding the war in North Germany showed the circulation of the issuing banks to be 39,875,000 L., and the deposits to be 6,472,000 L. while the corresponding figures at the present moment arecirculation, 60,000,000 L. and deposits 8,000,000 L. It would be idle to multiply Instances.

The reason why the use of bank paper commonly precedes the habit of making deposits in banks is very plain. It is a far easier habit to establish. In the issue of notes the banker, the person to be most benefited, can do something. He can pay away his own 'promises' in loans, in wages, or in payment of debts. But in the getting of deposits he is passive. His issues depend on himself; his deposits on the favour of others. And to the public the change is far easier too. To collect a great mass of deposits with the same banker, a great number of persons must agree to do something. But to establish a note circulation, a large number of persons need only do nothing. They receive the banker's notes in the common course of their business, and they have only not to take those notes to the banker for payment. If the public refrain from taking trouble, a paper circulation is immediately in existence. A paper circulation is begun by the banker, and requires no effort on the part of the public; on the contrary, it needs an effort of the public to be rid of notes once issued; but deposit banking cannot be begun by the banker, and requires a spontaneous and consistent effort in the community. And therefore paper issue is the natural prelude to deposit banking.

The way in which the issue of notes by a banker prepares the way for the deposit of money with him is very plain. When a private person

45

begins to possess a great heap of bank-notes, it will soon strike him that he is trusting the banker very much, and that in re turn he is getting nothing. He runs the risk of loss and robbery just as if he were hoarding coin. He would run no more risk by the failure of the bank if he made a deposit there, and he would be free from the risk of keeping the cash. No doubt it takes time before even this simple reasoning is understood by uneducated minds. So strong is the wish of most people to see their money that they for some time continue to hoard bank-notes: for a long period a few do so. But in the end common sense conquers. The circulation of bank-notes decreases, and the deposit of money with the banker increases. The credit of the banker having been efficiently advertised by the note, and accepted by the public, he lives on the credit so gained years after the note issue itself has ceased to be very important to him.

The efficiency of this introduction is proportional to the diffusion of the right of note issue. A single monopolist issuer, like the Bank of France, works its way with difficulty through a country, and advertises banking very slowly. Even now the Bank of France, which, I believe, by law ought to have a branch in each Department, has only branches in sixty out of eighty-six. On the other hand, the Swiss banks, where there is always one or more to every Canton, diffuse banking rapidly. We have seen that the liabilities of the Bank of France stand thus:

Notes L 112,000,000
Deposits L 15,000,000

But the aggregate Swiss banks, on the contrary, stand:

Notes L 761,000
Deposits L 4,709,000

The reason is that a central bank which is governed in the capital and descends on a country district, has much fewer modes of lending money safely than a bank of which the partners belong to that district, and know the men and things in it. A note issue is mainly begun by loans; there are then no deposits to be paid. But the mass of loans in a rural district are of small amount; the bills to be discounted are trifling; the persons borrowing are of small means and only local repute; the value of any property they wish to pledge depends on local changes and local circumstances. A banker who lives in the district, who has always lived there, whose whole mind is a history of the district and its changes, is easily able to lend money safely there. But a manager deputed by a single central establishment does so with difficulty. The worst people will come to him and ask for loans. His ignorance is a mark for all the shrewd and crafty people thereabouts. He will have endless difficulties in establishing the circulation of the distant bank, because he has not the local knowledge which alone can teach him how to issue that circulation with safety.

A system of note issues is therefore the best introduction to a large system of deposit banking. As yet, historically, it is the only introduction: no nation as yet has arrived at a great system of deposit banking without going first through the preliminary stage of note issue, and of such note issues the quickest and most efficient in this way is one made by individuals resident in the district, and conversant with it.

And this explains why deposit banking is so rare. Such a note issue as has been described is possible only in a country exempt from invasion, and free from revolution. During an invasion note-issuing banks must stop payment; a run is nearly inevitable at such a time, and in a revolution too. In such great and close civil dangers a nation is always demoralised; everyone looks to himself, and everyone likes to possess himself of the precious metals. These are sure to be valuable, invasion or no invasion, revolution or no revolution. But the goodness of bank-notes depends on the solvency of the banker, and that solvency may be impaired if the invasion is not repelled or the revolution resisted.

Hardly any continental country has been till now exempt for long periods both from invasion and revolution. In Holland and Germanytwo countries where note issue and deposit banking would seem as natural as in England and Scotlandthere was never any security from foreign war. A profound apprehension of external invasion penetrated their whole habits, and men of business would have thought it insane not to contemplate a contingency so frequent in their history, and perhaps witnessed by themselves.

France indeed, before 1789, was an exception. For many years under the old regime she was exempt from serious invasion or attempted revolution. Her Government was fixed, as was then thought, and powerful; it could resist any external enemy, and the prestige on which it rested seemed too firm to fear any enemy from within. But then it was not an honest Government, and it had shown its dishonesty in this particular matter of note issue. The regent in Law's time had given a monopoly of note issue to a bad bank, and had paid off the debts of the nation in worthiess paper. The Government had created a machinery of ruin, and had thriven on it. Among so apprehensive a race as the French the result was fatal. For many years no attempt at note issue or deposit banking was possible in France. So late as the foundation of the Caisse d'Escompte, in Turgot's time, the remembrance of Law's failure was distinctly felt, and impeded the commencement of better attempts.

This therefore is the reason why Lombard Street exists; that is, why England is a very great Money Market, and other European countries but small ones in comparison. In England and Scotland a diffused system of note issues started banks all over the country; in these banks the savings of the country have been lodged, and by these they have been sent to London. No similar system arose elsewhere, and in consequence London is full of money, and all continental cities are empty as compared with it.

47

II.

The monarchical form of Lombard Street is due also to the note issue. The origin of the Bank of England has been told by Macaulay, and it is never wise for an ordinary writer to tell again what he has told so much better. Nor is it necessary, for his writings are in everyone s hands. Still I must remind my readers of the curious story.

Of all institutions in the world the Bank of England is now probably the most remote from party politics and from 'financing.' But in its origin it was not only a finance company, but a Whig finance company. It was founded by a Whig Government because it was in desperate want of money, and supported by the 'City' because the 'City' was Whig. Very briefly, the story was this. The Government of Charles II. (under the Cabal Ministry) had brought the credit of the English State to the lowest possible point. It had perpetrated one of those monstrous frauds, which are likewise gross blunders. The goldsmiths, who then carried on upon a trifling scale what we should now call banking, used to deposit their reserve of treasure in the 'Exchequer,' with the sanction and under the care of the Government. In many European countries the credit of the State had been so much better than any other credit, that it had been used to strengthen the beginnings of banking. The credit of the state had been so used in England: though there had lately been a civil war and several revolutions, the honesty of the English Government was trusted implicitly. But Charles II. showed that it was trusted undeservedly. He shut up the 'Exchequer,' would pay no one, and so the 'goldsmiths' were ruined.

The credit of the Stuart Government never recovered from this monstrous robbery, and the Government created by the Revolution of 1688 could hardly expect to be more trusted with money than its predecessor. A Government created by a revolution hardly ever is. There is a taint of violence which capitalists dread instinctively, and there is always a rational apprehension that the Government which one revolution thought fit to set up another revolution may think fit to pull down. In 1694, the credit of William III.'s Government was so low in London that it was impossible for it to borrow any large sum; and the evil was the greater, because in consequence of the French war the financial straits of the Government were extreme. At last a scheme was hit upon which would relieve their necessities. 'The plan,' says Macaulay, 'was that twelve hundred thousand pounds should be raised at what was then considered as the moderate rate of 8 per cent.' In order to induce the subscribers to advance the money promptly on terms so unfavourable to the public, the subscribers were to be incorporated by the name of the Governor and Company of the Bank of England. They were so incorporated, and the 1,200,000 L. was obtained.

On many succeeding occasions, their credit was of essential use to the Government. Without their aid, our National Debt could not have been borrowed; and if we had not been able to raise that money we should have been conquered by France and compelled to take back James II. And for many years afterwards the existence of that debt was a main reason why the industrial classes never would think of recalling the Pretender, or of upsetting the revolution settlement. The 'fund-holder' is always considered in the books of that time as opposed to his 'legitimate' sovereign, because it was to be feared that this sovereign would repudiate the debt which was raised by those who dethroned him, and which was spent in resisting him and his allies. For a long time the Bank of England was the focus of London Liberalism, and in that capacity rendered to the State inestimable services. In return for these substantial benefits the Bank of England received from the Government, either at first or afterwards, three most important privileges.

First. The Bank of England had the exclusive possession of the Government balances. In its first period, as I have shown, the Bank gave credit to the Government, but afterwards it derived credit from the Government. There is a natural tendency in men to follow the example of the Government under which they live. The Government is the largest, most important, and most conspicuous entity with which the mass of any people are acquainted; its range of knowledge must always be infinitely greater than the average of their knowledge, and therefore, unless there is a conspicuous warning to the contrary, most men are inclined to think their Government right, and, when they can, to do what it does. Especially in money matters a man might fairly reason'If the Government is right in trusting the Bank of England with the great balance of the nation, I cannot be wrong in trusting it with my little balance.'

Second. The Bank of England had, till lately, the monopoly of limited liability in England. The common law of England knows nothing of any such principle. It is only possible by Royal Charter or Statute Law. And by neither of these was any real bank (I do not count absurd schemes such as Chamberlayne's Land Bank) permitted with limited liability in England till within these few years. Indeed, a good many people thought it was right for the Bank of England, but not right for any other bank. I remember hearing the conversation of a distinguished merchant in the City of London, who well represented the ideas then most current He was declaiming against banks of limited liability, and some one asked'Why, what do you say, then, to the Bank of England, where you keep your own account?' 'Oh!' he replied, 'that is an exceptional case.' And no doubt it was an exception of the greatest value to the Bank of England, because it induced many quiet and careful merchants to be directors of the Bank, who certainly would not have joined any bank where all their fortunes were liable, and where the liability was not limited.

Thirdly. The Bank of England had the privilege of being the sole joint stock company permitted to issue bank notes in England. Private London bankers did indeed issue notes down to the middle of the last century, but no joint stock company could do so. The explanatory clause of the Act of 1742 sounds most curiously to our modern ears. 'And to prevent any doubt that may arise concerning the privilege or power given to the said governor and company' that is, the Bank of England' OF EXCLUSIVE BANKING; and also in regard to creating any other bank or banks by Parliament, or restraining other persons from banking during the continuance of the said privilege granted to the governor and company of the Bank of England, as before recited; it is hereby further enacted and declared by the authority aforesaid, that it is the true intent and meaning of the said Act that no other bank shall be created, established, or allowed by Parliament, and that it shall not be lawful for any body politic or corporate whatsoever created or to be created, or for any other persons whatsoever united or to be united in covenants or partnership exceeding the number of six persons in that part of Great Britain called England, to borrow, owe, or take up any sum or sums of money on their bills or notes payable on demand or at any less time than six months from the borrowing thereof during the continuance of such said privilege to the said governor and company, who are hereby declared to be and remain a corporation with the privilege of exclusive banking, as before recited.' To our modern ears these words seem to mean more than they did. The term banking was then applied only to the issue of notes and the taking up of money on bills on demand. Our present system of deposit banking, in which no bills or promissory notes are issued, was not then known on a great scale, and was not called banking. But its effect was very important. It in time gave the Bank of England the monopoly of the note issue of the Metropolis. It had at that time no branches, and so it did not compete for the country circulation. But in the Metropolis, where it did compete, it was completely victorious. No company but the Bank of England could issue notes, and unincorporated individuals gradually gave way, and ceased to do so. Up to 1844 London private bankers might have issued notes if they pleased, but almost a hundred years ago they were forced out of the field. The Bank of England has so long had a practical monopoly of the circulation, that it is commonly believed always to have had a legal monopoly.

And the practical effect of the clause went further: it was believed to make the Bank of England the only joint stock company that could receive deposits, as well as the only company that could issue notes. The gift of 'exclusive banking' to the Bank of England was read in its most natural modern sense: it was thought to prohibit any other banking company from carrying on our present system of banking. After joint stock banking was permitted in the country, people began to inquire why it should not exist in the Metropolis too? And then it was seen that the words I have quoted only forbid the issue of negotiable instruments, and not the receiving of money when no such instrument is given. Upon this construction, the London and Westminster Bank and all our older joint stock banks were founded. But till they began, the Bank of England had among companies not only the exclusive privilege of note issue, but that of deposit banking too. It was in every sense the only banking company in London.

With so many advantages over all competitors, it is quite natural that the Bank of England should have far outstripped them all. Inevitably it became the bank in London; all the other bankers grouped themselves round it, and lodged their reserve with it. Thus our one reserve system of banking was not deliberately founded upon definite reasons; it was the gradual consequence of many singular events, and of an accumulation of legal privileges on a single bank which has now been altered, and which no one would now defend.

CHAPTER IV.

The Position of the Chancellor of the Exchequer in the Money Market.

Nothing can be truer in theory than the economical principle that banking is a trade and only a trade, and nothing can be more surely established by a larger experience than that a Government which interferes with any trade injuries that trade. The best thing undeniably that a Government can do with the Money Market is to let it take care of itself.

But a Government can only carry out this principle universally if it observe one condition: it must keep its own money. The Government is necessarily at times possessed of large sums in cash. It is by far the richest corporation in the country; its annual revenue payable in money far surpasses that of any other body or person. And if it begins to deposit this immense income as it accrues at any bank, at once it becomes interested in the welfare of that bank. It cannot pay the interest on its debt if that bank cannot produce the public deposits when that interest becomes due; it cannot pay its salaries, and defray its miscellaneous expenses, if that bank fail at any time. A modern Government is like a very rich man with very great debts which he cannot well pay; its credit is necessary to its prosperity, almost to its existence, and if its banker fail when one of its debts becomes due its difficulty is intense.

Another banker, it will be said, may take up the Government account. He may advance, as is so often done in other bank failures, what the Government needs for the moment in order to secure the Government account in future. But the imperfection of this remedy is that it fails in the very worst case. In a panic, and at a general collapse of credit, no such banker will probably be found. The old banker who possesses the Government deposit cannot repay it, and no banker not having that deposit will, at a bad crisis, be able to find the 5,000,000 L. or 6,000,000 L. which the quarter day of a Government such as ours requires. If a finance Minister, having entrusted his money to a bank, begins to act strictly, and say he will in all cases let the Money Market take care of itself, the reply is that in one case the Money Market will take care of him too, and he will be insolvent.

In the infancy of Banking it is probably much better that a Government should as a rule keep its own money. If there are not Banks in which it can place secure reliance, it should not seem to rely upon them. Still less should it give peculiar favour to any one, and by entrusting it with the Government account secure to it a mischievous supremacy above all other banks. The skill of a financier in such an age is to equalise the receipt of taxation, and the outgoing of expenditure; it should be a principal care with him to make sure that more should not be locked up at a particular moment in the Government coffers than is usually locked up there. If the amount of dead capital so buried in the Treasury does not at any time much exceed the common average, the evil so caused is inconsiderable: it is only the loss of interest on a certain sum of money, which would not be much of a burden on the whole nation; the additional taxation it would cause would be inconsiderable. Such an evil is nothing in comparison with that of losing the money necessary for inevitable expence by entrusting it to a bad Bank, or that of recovering this money by identifying the national credit with the bad Bank and so propping it up and perpetuating it. So long as the security of the Money Market is not entirely to be relied on, the Goverment of a country had much better leave it to itself and keep its own money. If the banks are bad, they will certainly continue bad and will probably become worse if the Government sustains and encourages them. The cardinal maxim is, that any aid to a present bad Bank is the surest mode of preventing the establishment of a future good Bank.

When the trade of Banking began to be better understood, when the Banking system was thoroughly secure, the Government might begin to lend gradually; especially to lend the unusually large sums which even under the most equable system of finance will at times accumulate in the public exchequer.

Under a natural system of banking it would have every facility. Where there were many banks keeping their own reserve, and each most anxious to keep a sufficient reserve, because its own life and credit depended on it, the risk of the Government in keeping a banker would be reduced to a minimum. It would have the choice of many bankers, and would not be restricted to any one.

Its course would be very simple, and be analogous to that of other public bodies in the country. The Metropolitan Board of Works, which collects a great revenue in London, has an account at the London and Westminster Bank, for which that bank makes a deposit of Consols as a security. The Chancellor of the Exchequer would have no difficulty in getting such security either. If, as is likely, his account would be thought to be larger than any single bank ought to be entrusted with, the public deposits might be divided between several. Each would give security, and the whole public money would be safe. If at any time the floating money in the hands of Government were exceptionally large, he might require augmented security to be lodged, and he might obtain an interest. He would be a lender of such magnitude and so much influence, that he might command his own terms. He might get his account kept safe if anyone could.

If, on the other hand, the Chancellor of the Exchequer were a borrower, as at times he is, he would have every facility in obtaining what he wanted. The credit of the English Government is so good that he could borrow better than anyone else in the world. He would have greater facility, indeed, than now, for, except with the leave of Parliament, the Chancellor of the Exchequer cannot borrow by our present laws in the open market. He can only borrow from the Bank of England on what are called 'deficiency bills.' In a natural system, he would borrow of any one out of many competing banks, selecting the one that would lend cheapest; but under our present artificial system, he is confined to a single bank, which can fix its own charge.

If contrary to expectation a collapse occurred, the Government might withdraw, as the American Government actually has withdrawn, its balance from the bankers. It might give its aid, lend Exchequer bills, or otherwise pledge its credit for the moment, but when the exigency was passed it might let the offending banks suffer. There would be a penalty for their misconduct. New and better banks, who might take warning from that misconduct, would arise. As in all natural trades, what is old and, rotten would perish, what is new and good would replace it. And till the new banks had proved, by good conduct, their fitness for State confidence, the State need not give it. The Government could use its favour as a bounty on pmdence, and the withdrawal of that favour as a punishment for culpable folly.

Under a good system of banking, a great collapse, except from rebellion or invasion, would probably not happen. A large number of banks, each feeling that their credit was at stake in keeping a good reserve, probably would keep one; if any one did not, it would be criticised constantly, and would soon lose its standing, and in the end disappear. And such banks would meet an incipient panic freely, and generously; they would advance out of their reserve boldly and largely, for each individual bank would fear suspicion, and know that at such periods it must 'show strength,' if at such times it wishes to be thought to have strength. Such a system reduces to a minimum the risk that is caused by the deposit. If the national money can safely be deposited in banks in any way, this is the way to make it safe.

But this system is nearly the opposite to that which the law and circumstances have created for us in England. The English Government, far from keeping cash from the money market till the position of that market was reasonably secure, at a very early moment, and while credit of all kinds was most insecure, for its own interests entered into the Money Market. In order to effect loans better, it gave the custody and profit of its own money (along with other privileges) to a single bank, and therefore practically and in fact it is identified with the Bank of this hour. It cannot let the money market take care of itself because it has deposited much money in that market, and it cannot pay its way if it loses that money.

Nor would any English statesman propose to 'wind up' the Bank of England. A theorist might put such a suggestion on paper, but no responsible government would think of it. At the worst crisis and in the worst misconduct of the Bank, no such plea has been thought of: in 1825 when its till was empty, in 1837 when it had to ask aid from the Bank of France, no such idea was suggested. By irresistible tradition the English Government was obliged to deposit its money in the money market and to deposit with this particular Bank.

And this system has plain and grave evils.

1st. Because being created by state aid, it is more likely than a natural system to require state help.

2ndly. Because, being a one-reserve system, it reduces the spare cash of the Money Market to a smaller amount than any other system, and so makes that market more delicate. There being a less hoard to meet liabilities, any error in the management of that reserve has a proportionately greater effect.

3rdly. Because, our one reserve is, by the necessity of its nature, given over to one board of directors, and we are therefore dependent on the wisdom of that one only, and cannot, as in most trades, strike an average of the wisdom and the folly, the discretion and the indiscretion, of many competitors.

Lastly. Because that board of directors is, like every other board, pressed on by its shareholders to make a high dividend, and therefore to keep a small reserve, whereas the public interest imperatively requires that they shall keep a large one.

These four evils were inseparable from the system, but there is besides an additional and accidental evil. The English Government not only created this singular system, but it proceeded to impair it, and demoralise all the public opinion respecting it. For more than a century after its creation (notwithstanding occasional errors) the Bank of England, in the main, acted with judgment and with caution. Its business was but small as we should now reckon, but for the most part it conducted that business with prudence and discretion. In 1696, it had been involved in the most serious difficulties, and had been obliged to refuse to pay some of its notes. For a long period it was in wholesome dread of public opinion, and the necessity of retaining public confidence made it cautious. But the English Government removed that necessity. In 1797, Mr. Pitt feared that he might not be able to obtain sufficient species for foreign payments, in consequence of the low state of the Bank reserve, and he therefore required the Bank not to pay in cash. He removed the preservative apprehension which is the best security of all Banks.

For this reason the period under which the Bank of England did not pay gold for its notes--the period from 1797 to 1819--is always called the period of the Bank restriction. As the Bank during that period did not perform, and was not compelled by law to perform, its contract of paying its notes in cash, it might apparently have been well called the period of Bank license. But the word 'restriction' was quite right, and was the only proper word as a description of, the policy of 1797. Mr. Pitt did not say that the Bank of England need not pay its notes in specie; he 'restricted' them from doing so; he said that they must not.

In consequence, from 1797 to 1844 (when a new era begins), there never was a proper caution on the part of the Bank directors. At heart they considered that the Bank of England had a kind of charmed life, and that it was above the ordinary banking anxiety to pay its way. And this feeling was very natural. A bank of issue, which need not pay its notes in cash, has a charmed life; it can lend what it wishes, and issue what it likes, with no fear of harm to itself, and with no substantial check but its own inclination. For nearly a quarter of a century, the Bank of England was such a bank, for all that time it could not be in any danger. And naturally the public mind was demoralised also. Since 1797, the public have always expected the Government to help the Bank if necessary. I cannot fully discuss the suspensions of the Act of 1844 in 1847, 1857, and 1866; but indisputably one of their effects is to make people think that Government will always help the Bank if the Bank is in extremity. And this is the sort of anticipation which tends to justify itself, and to cause what it expects.

On the whole, therefore, the position of the Chancellor of the Exchequer in our Money Market is that of one who deposits largely in it, who created it, and who demoralised it. He cannot, therefore, banish it from his thoughts, or decline responsibility for it. He must arrange his finances so as not to intensify panics, but to mitigate them. He must aid the Bank of England in the discharge of its duties; he must not impede or prevent it.

His aid may be most efficient. He is, on finance, the natural exponent of the public opinion of England. And it is by that opinion that we wish the Bank of England to be guided. Under a natural system of banking we should have relied on self-interest, but the State prevented that; we now rely on opinion instead; the public approval is a reward, its disapproval a severe penalty, on the Bank directors; and of these it is most important that the finance minister should be a sound and felicitous exponent.

CHAPTER V.

The Mode in Which the Value of Money Is Settled in Lombard Street.

Many persons believe that the Bank of England has some peculiar power of fixing the value of money. They see that the Bank of England varies its minimum rate of discount from time to time, and that, more or less, all other banks follow its lead, and charge much as it charges; and they are puzzled why this should be. 'Money,' as economists teach, 'is a commodity, and only a commodity;' why then, it is asked, is its value fixed in so odd a way, and not the way in which the value of all other commodities is fixed?

There is at bottom, however, no difficulty in the matter. The value of money is settled, like that of all other commodities, by supply and demand, and only the form is essentially different. In other commodities all the large dealers fix their own price; they try to underbid one another, and that keeps down the price; they try to get as much as they can out of the buyer, and that keeps up the price. Between the two what Adam Smith calls the higgling of the market settles it. And this is the most simple and natural mode of doing business, but it is not the only mode. If circumstances make it convenient another may be adopted. A single large holder--especially if he be by far the greatest holder--may fix his price, and other dealers may say whether or not they will undersell him, or whether or not they will ask more than he does. A very considerable holder of an article may, for a time, vitally affect its value if he lay down the minimum price which he will take, and obstinately adhere to it. This is the way in which the value of money in Lombard Street is settled. The Bank of England used to be a predominant, and is still a most important, dealer in money. It lays down the least price at which alone it will dispose of its stock, and this, for the most part, enables other dealers to obtain that price, or something near it.

The reason is obvious. At all ordinary moments there is not money enough in Lombard Street to discount all the bills in Lombard Street without taking some money from the Bank of England. As soon as the Bank rate is fixed, a great many persons who have bills to discount try how much cheaper than the Bank they can get these bills discounted. But they seldom can get them discounted very much cheaper, for if they did everyone would leave the Bank, and the outer market would have more bills than it could bear.

In practice, when the Bank finds this process beginning, and sees that its business is much diminishing, it lowers the rate, so as to secure a reasonable portion of the business to itself, and to keep a fair part of its deposits employed. At Dutch auctions an upset or maximum price used to be fixed by the seller, and he came down in his bidding till he found a buyer. The value of money is fixed in Lombard Street in much the same way, only that the upset price is not that of all sellers, but that of one very important seller, some part of whose supply is essential.

The notion that the Bank of England has a control over the Money Market, and can fix the rate of discount as it likes, has survived from the old days before 1844, when the Bank could issue as many notes as it liked. But even then the notion was a mistake. A bank with a monopoly of note issue has great sudden power in the Money Market, but no permanent power: it can affect the rate of discount at any particular moment, but it cannot affect the average rate. And the reason is, that any momentary fall in money, caused by the caprice of such a bank, of itself tends to create an immediate and equal rise, so that upon an average the value is not altered.

What happens is this. If a bank with a monopoly of note issue suddenly lends (suppose) 2,000,000 L. more than usual, it causes a proportionate increase of trade and increase of prices. The persons to whom that 2,000,000 L. was lent, did not borrow it to lock it up; they borrow it, in the language of the market, to 'operate with' that is, they try to buy with it; and that new attempt to buythat new demand raises prices. And this rise of prices has three consequences. First. It makes everybody else want to borrow money. Money is not so efficient in buying as it was, and therefore operators require more money for the same dealings. If railway stock is 10 per cent dearer this year than last, a speculator who borrows money to enable him to deal must borrow 0 per cent more this year than last, and in consequence there is an augmented demand for loans. Secondly. This is an effectual demand, for the increased price of railway stock enables those who wish it to borrow more upon it. The common practice is to lend a certain portion of the market value of such securities, and if that value increases, the amount of the usual loan to be obtained on them increases too. In this way, therefore, any artificial reduction in the value of money causes a new augmentation of the demand for money, and thus restores that value to its natural level. In all business this is well known by experience: a stimulated market soon becomes a tight market, for so sanguine are enterprising men, that as soon as they get any unusual ease they always fancy that the relaxation is greater than it is, and speculate till they want more than they can obtain.

In these two ways sudden loans by an issuer of notes, though they may temporarily lower the value of money, do not lower it permanently, because they generate their own counteraction. And this they do whether the notes issued are convertible into coin or not. During the period of Bank restriction, from 1797 to 1819, the Bank of England could not absolutely control the Money Market, any more than it could after 1819, when it was compelled to pay its notes in coin. But in the case of convertible notes there is a third effect, which works in the same direction, and works more quickly. A rise of prices, confined to one country, tends to increase imports, because other countries can obtain more for their goods if they send them there, and it discourages exports, because a merchant who would have gained a profit before the rise by buying here to sell again will not gain so much, if any, profit after that rise. By this augmentation of imports the indebtedness of this country is augmented, and by this diminution of exports the proportion of that indebtedness which is paid in the usual way is decreased also. In consequence, there is a larger balance to be paid in bullion; the store in the bank or banks keeping the reserve is diminished, and the rate of interest must be raised by them to stay the effiux. And the tightness so produced is often greater than, and always equal to, the preceding unnatural laxity.

There is, therefore, no ground for believing, as is so common, that the value of money is settled by different causes than those which affect the value of other commodities, or that the Bank of England has any despotism in that matter. It has the power of a large holder of money, and no more. Even formerly, when its monetary powers were greater and its rivals weaker, it had no absolute control. It was simply a large corporate dealer, making bids and much influencing though in no sense compellingother dealers thereby.

But though the value of money is not settled in an exceptional way, there is nevertheless a peculiarity about it, as there is about many articles. It is a commodity subject to great fluctuations of value, and those fluctuations are easily produced by a slight excess or a slight deficiency of quantity. Up to a certain point money is a necessity. If a merchant has acceptances to meet to-morrow, money he must and will find today at some price or other. And it is this urgent need of the whole body of merchants which runs up the value of money so wildly and to such a height in a great panic. On the other hand, money easily becomes a 'drug,' as the phrase is, and there is soon too much of it. The number of accepted securities is limited, and cannot be rapidly increased; if the amount of money seeking these accepted securities is more than can be lent on them the value of money soon goes down. You may often hear in the market that bills are not to be had, meaning good bills of course, and when you hear this you may be sure that the value of money is very low.

If money were all held by the owners of it, or by banks which did not pay an interest for it, the value of money might not fall so fast. Money would, in the market phrase, be 'well held.' The possessors would be under no necessity to employ it all; they might employ part at a high rate rather than all at a low rate. But in Lombard Street money is very largely held by those who do pay an interest for it, and such persons must employ it all, or almost all, for they have much to pay out with one hand, and unless they receive much with the other they will be ruined. Such persons do not so much care what is the rate of interest at which they employ their money: they can reduce the interest they pay in proportion to that which they can make. The vital points to them is to employ it at some rate. If you hold (as in Lombard Street some persons do) millions of other people's money at interest, arithmetic teaches that you will soon be ruined if you make nothing of it even if the interest you pay is not high.

The fluctuations in the value of money are therefore greater than those on the value of most other commodities. At times there is an excessive pressure to borrow it, and at times an excessive pressure to lend it, and so the price is forced up and down.

These considerations enable us to estimate the responsibility which is thrown on the Bank of England by our system, and by every system on the bank or banks who by it keep the reserve of bullion or of legal tender exchangeable for bullion. These banks can in no degree control the permanent value of money, but they can completely control its momentary value. They cannot change the average value, but they can determine the deviations from the average. If the dominant banks manage ill, the rate of interest will at one time be excessively high, and at another time excessively low: there will be first a pernicious excitement, and next a fatal collapse. But if they manage well, the rate of interest will not deviate so much from the average rate; it will neither ascend so high nor descend so low. As far as anything can be steady the value of money will then be steady, and probably in consequence trade will be steady tooat least a principal cause of periodical disturbance will have been withdrawn from it.

CHAPTER VI.

Why Lombard Street Is Often Very Dull, and Sometimes Extremely Excited.

Any sudden event which creates a great demand for actual cash may cause, and will tend to cause, a panic in a country where cash is much economised, and where debts payable on demand are large. In such a country an immense credit rests on a small cash reserve, and an unexpected and large diminution of that reserve may easily break up and shatter very much, if not the whole, of that credit. Such accidental events are of the most various nature: a bad harvest, an apprehension of foreign invasion, the sudden failure of a great firm which everybody trusted, and many other similar events, have all caused a sudden demand for cash. And some writers have endeavoured to classify panics according to the nature of the particular accidents producing them. But little, however, is, I believe, to be gained by such classifications. There is little difference in the effect of one accident and another upon our credit system. We must be prepared for all of them, and we must prepare for all of them in the same wayby keeping a large cash reserve.

But it is of great importance to point out that our industrial organisation is liable not only to irregnlar external accidents, but likewise to regnlar internal changes; that these changes make our credit system much more delicate at some times than at others; and that it is the recurrence of these periodical seasons of delicacy which has given rise to the notion that panics come according to a fixed rule, that every ten years or so we must have one of them.

Most persons who begin to think of the subject are puzzled on the threshold. They hear much of 'good times' and 'bad times,' meaning by 'good' times in which nearly everyone is very well off, and by 'bad' times in which nearly everyone is comparatively ill off. And at first it is natural to ask why should everybody, or almost everybody, be well off together? Why should there be any great tides of industry, with large diffused profit by way of flow, and large diffused want of profit, or loss, by way of ebb? The main answer is hardly given distinctly in our common books of political economy. These books do not tell you what is the fund out of which large general profits are paid in good times, nor do they ex plain why that fund is not available for the same purpose in

63

bad times. Our current political economy does not sufficiently take account of time as an element in trade operations; but as soon as the division of labour has once established itself in a community, two principles at once begin to be important, of which time is the very essence. These are

First. That as goods are produced to be exchanged, it is good that they should be exchanged as quickly as possible.

Secondly. That as every producer is mainly occupied in producing what others want, and not what he wants himself, it is desirable that he should always be able to find, without effort, without delay, and without uncertainty, others who want what he can produce.

In themselves these principles are self-evident. Everyone will admit it to be expedient that all goods wanting to be sold should be sold as soon as they are ready; that every man who wants to work should find employment as soon as he is ready for it. Obviously also, as soon as the 'division of labour' is really established, there is a difficulty about both of these principles. A produces what he thinks B wants, but it may be a mistake, and B may not want it. A may be able and willing to produce what B wants, but he may not be able to find Bhe may not know of his existence.

The general truth of these principles is obvious, but what is not obvious is the extreme greatness of their effects. Taken together, they make the whole difference between times of brisk trade and great prosperity, and times of stagnant trade and great adversity, so far as that prosperity and that adversity are real and not illusory. If they are satisfied, everyone knows whom to work for, and what to make, and he can get immediately in exchange what he wants'himself. There is no idle labour and no sluggish capital in the whole community, and, in consequence, all which can be produced is produced, the effectiveness of human industry is augmented, and both kinds of producers both capitalists and labourersare much richer than usual, because the amount to be divided between them is also much greater than usual.

And there is a partnership in industries. No single large industry can be depressed without injury to other industries; still less can any great group of industries. Each industry when prosperous buys and consumes the produce probably of most (certainly of very many) other industries, and if industry A fail and is in difficulty, industries B, and C, and D, which used to sell to it, will not be able to sell that which they had produced in reliance on A's demand, and in future they will stand idle till industry A recovers, because in default of A there will be no one to buy the commodities which they create. Then as industry B buys of C, D, &c., the adversity of B tells on C, D, &c., and as these buy of E, F, &c., the effect is propagated through the whole alphabet. And in a certain sense it rebounds. Z feels the want caused by the diminished custom of A, B, & C, and so it does not earn so much; in consequence, it cannot lay out as much on the produce of A, B, & C, and so these do not earn as much either. In all this money is but an instrument. The same thing would happen equally well in a trade of barter, if a state of barter on a very large scale were not practically impossible, on account of the time and trouble which it would necessarily require. As has been explained, the fundamental cause is that under a system in which everyone is dependent on the labour of everyone else, the loss of one spreads and multiplies through all, and spreads and multiplies the faster the higher the previous perfection of the system of divided labour, and the more nice and effectual the mode of interchange. And the entire effect of a depression in any single large trade requires a considerable time before it can be produced. It has to be propagated, and to be returned through a variety of industries, before it is complete. Short depressions, in consequence, have scarcely any discernible consequences; they are over before we think of their effects. It is only in the case of continuous and considerable depressions that the cause is in action long enough to produce discernible effects.

The most common, and by far the most important, case where the depression in one trade causes depression in all others, is that of depressed agriculture. When the agriculture of the world is ill off, food is dear. And as the amount of absolute necessaries which a people consumes cannot be much diminished, the additional amount which has to be spent on them is so much subtracted from what used to be spent on other things. All the industries, A, B, C, D, up to Z, are somewhat affected by an augmentation in the price of corn, and the most affected are the large ones, which produce the objects in ordinary times most consumed by the working classes. The clothing trades feel the difference at once, and in this country the liquor trade (a great source of English revenue) feels it almost equally soon. Especially when for two or three years harvests have been bad, and corn has long been dear, every industry is impoverished, and almost every one, by becoming poorer, makes every other poorer too. All trades are slack from diminished custom, and the consequence is a vast stagnant capital, much idle labour, and a greatly retarded production.

It takes two or three years to produce this full calamity, and the recovery from it takes two or three years also. If corn should long be cheap, the labouring classes have much to spend on what they like besides. The producers of those things become prosperous, and have a greater purchasing power. They exercise it, and that creates in the class they deal with another purchasing power, and so all through society. The whole machine of industry is stimulated to its maximum of energy, just as before much of it was slackened almost to its minimum.

A great calamity to any great industry will tend to produce the same effect, but the fortunes of the industries on which the wages of labour are expended are much more important than those of all others, because they act much more quickly upon a larger mass of purchasers. On principle, if there was a perfect division of labour, every industry would have to be perfectly prosperous in order that any one might be so. So far, therefore, from its being at all natural that trade should develop constantly, steadily, and equably, it is plain, without going farther, from theory as well as from experience, that there are inevitably periods of rapid dilatation, and as inevitably periods of contraction and of stagnation.

Nor is this the only changeable element in modern industrial societies. Credit--the disposition of one man to trust another--is singularly varying. In England, after a great calamity, everybody is suspicious of everybody; as soon as that calamity is forgotten, everybody again confides in everybody. On the Continent there has been a stiff controversy as to whether credit should or should not be called capital:' in England, even the little attention once paid to abstract economics is now diverted, and no one cares in the least for refined questions of this kind: the material practical point is that, in M. Chevalier's language, credit is 'additive,' or additionalthat is, in times when credit is good productive power is more efficient, and in times when credit is bad productive power is less efficient. And the state of credit is thus influential, because of the two principles which have just been explained. In a good state of credit, goods lie on hand a much less time than when credit is bad; sales are quicker; intermediate dealers borrow easily to augment their trade, and so more and more goods are more quickly and more easily transmitted from the producer to the consumer.

These two variable causes are causes of real prosperity. They augment trade and production, and so are plainly beneficial, except where by mistake the wrong things are produced, or where also by mistake misplaced credit is given, and a man who cannot produce anything which is wanted gets the produce of other people's labour upon a false idea that he will produce it. But there is another variable cause which produces far more of apparent than of real prosperity and of which the effect is in actual life mostly confused with those of the others.

In our common speculations we do not enough remember that interest on money is a refined idea, and not a universal one. So far indeed is it from being universal, that the majority of saving persons in most countries would reject it. Most savings in most countries are held in hoarded specie. In Asia, in Africa, in South America, largely even in Europe, they are thus held, and it would frighten most of the owners to let them out of their keeping. An Englishman a modern Englishman at leastassumes as a first principle that he ought to be able to 'put his money into something safe that will yield 5 per cent;' but most saving persons in most countries are afraid to 'put their money' into anything. Nothing is safe to their minds; indeed, in most countries, owing to a bad Government and a backward industry, no investment, or hardly any, really is safe. In most countries most men are content to forego interest; but in more advanced countries, at some times there are more savings seeking investment than there are known investments for; at other times there is no such superabundance. Lord Macaulay has graphically described one of the periods of excess. He says'During the interval between the Restoration and the Revolution the riches of the nation had been rapidly increasing. Thousands of busy men found every Christmas that, after the expenses of the year's housekeeping had been defrayed out of the year's income, a surplus remained; and how that surplus was to be employed was a question of some difficulty. In our time, to invest such a surplus, at something more than three per cent, on the best security that has ever been known in the world, is the work of a few minutes. But in the seventeenth century, a lawyer, a physician, a retired merchant, who had saved some thousands, and who wished to place them safely and profitably, was often greatly embarrassed. Three generations earlier, a man who had accumulated wealth in a profession generally purchased real property, or lent his savings on mortgage. But the number of acres in the kingdom had remained the same; and the value of those acres, though it had greatly increased, had by no means increased so fast as the quantity of capital which was seeking for employment. Many too wished to put their money where they could find it at an hour's notice, and looked about for some species of property which could be more readily transferred than a house or a field. A capitalist might lend on bottomry or on personal security; but, if he did so, he ran a great risk of losing interest and principal. There were a few joint stock companies, among which the East India Company held the foremost place; but the demand for the stock of such companies was far greater than the supply. Indeed the cry for a new East India Company was chiefly raised by persons who had found difficulty in placing their savings at interest on good security. So great was that difficulty that the practice of hoarding was common. We are told that the father of Pope, the poet, who retired from business in the City about the time of the Revolution, carried to a retreat in the country a strong box containing near twenty thousand pounds, and took out from time to time what was required for household expenses; and it is highiy probable that this was not a solitary case. At present the quantity of coin which is hoarded by private persons is so small, that it would, if brought forth, make no perceptible addition to the circulation. But, in the earlier part of the reign of William the Third, all the greatest writers on currency were of opinion that a very considerable mass of gold and silver was hidden in secret drawers and behind wainscots.

'The natural effect of this state of things was that a crowd of projectors, ingenious and absurd, honest and knavish, employed themselves in devising new schemes for the employment of redundant capital. It was about the year 1688 that the word stockjobber was first heard in London. In the short space of four years a crowd of companies, every one of which confidently held out to subscribers the hope of immense gains, sprang into existence--the Insurance Company, the Paper Company, the Lutestring Company, the Pearl Fishery Company, the Glass Bottle Company, the Alum Company, the Blythe Coal Company, the Swordblade Company. There was a Tapestry Company, which would soon furnish pretty hangings for all the parlours of the middle class, and for all the bedchambers of the higher. There was a Copper Company, which proposed to explore the mines of England, and held out a hope that they would prove not less valuable than those of Potosi. There was a Diving Company, which undertook to bring up precious effects from shipwrecked vessels, and which announced that it had laid in a stock of wonderful machines resembling complete suits of armour. In front of the helmet was a huge glass eye like that of a Cyclops; and out of the crest went a pipe through which the air was to be admitted. The whole process was exhibited on the Thames. Fine gentlemen and fine ladies were invited to the show, were hospitably regaled, and were delighted by seeing the divers in their panoply descend into the river and return laden with old iron and ship's tackle. There was a Greenland Fishing Company, which could not fail to drive the Dutch whalers and herring busses out of the Northern Ocean. There was a Tanning Company, which promised to furnish leather superior to the best that was brought from Turkey or Russia. There was a society which undertook the office of giving gentlemen a liberal education on low terms, and which assumed the sounding name of the Royal Academies Company. In a pompous advertisement it was announced that the directors of the Royal Academies Company had engaged the best masters in every branch of knowledge, and were about to issue twenty thousand tickets at twenty shillings each. There was to be a lottery--two thousand prizes were to be drawn; and the fortunate holders of the prizes were to be taught, at the charge of the Company, Latin, Greek, Hebrew, French, Spanish, conic sections, trigonometry, heraldry, japaning, fortification, bookkeeping, and the art of playing the theorbo.'

The panic was forgotten till Lord Macaulay revived the memory of it. But, in fact, in the South Sea Bubble, which has always been remembered, the form was the same, only a little more extravagant; the companies in that mania were for objects such as these:--' "Wrecks to be fished for on the Irish Coast--Insurance of Horses and other Cattle (two millions)--Insurance of Losses by Servants--To make Salt Water Fresh--For building of Hospitals for Bastard Children--For building of Ships against Pirates--For making of Oil from Sun-flower Seeds--For improving of Malt Liquors--For recovery of Seamen's Wages--For extracting of Silver from Lead--For the transmuting of Quicksilver into a malleable and fine Metal--For making of Iron with Pit-coal--For importing a Number of large Jack Asses from Spain--For trading in Human Hair--For fatting of Hogs--For a Wheel of Perpetual Motion." But the most strange of all, perhaps, was "For an Undertaking which shall in due time be revealed." Each subscriber was to pay down two gnineas, and hereafter to receive a share of one hundred, with a disclosure of the object; and so tempting was the offer, that 1,000 of these subscriptions were paid the same morning, with which the projector went off in the afternoon.' In 1825 there were speculations in companies nearly as wild, and just before 1866 there were some of a like nature, though not equally extravagant. The fact is, that the owners of savings not finding, in adequate quantities, their usual kind of investments, rush into anything that promises speciously, and when they find that these specious investments can be disposed of at a high profit, they rush into them more and more. The first taste is for high interest, but that taste soon becomes secondary. There is a second appetite for large gains to be made by selling the principal which is to yield the interest. So long as such sales can be effected the mania continues; when it ceases to be possible to effect them, ruin begins.

So long as the savings remain in possession of their owners, these hazardous gamblings in speculative undertakings are almost the whole effect of an excess of accumulation over tested investment. Little effect is produced on the general trade of the country. The owners of the savings are too scattered and far from the market to change the majority of mercantile transactions. But when these savings come to be lodged in the hands of bankers, a much wider result is produced. Bankers are close to mercantile life; they are always ready to lend on good mercantile securities; they wish to lend on such securities a large part of the money entrusted to them. When, therefore, the money so entrusted is unusually large, and when it long continues so, the general trade of the country is, in the course of time, changed. Bankers are daily more and more ready to lend money to mercantile men; more is lent to such men; more bargains are made in consequence; commodities are more sought after; and, in consequence, prices rise more and more.

The rise of prices is quickest in an improving state of credit. Prices in general are mostly determined by wholesale transactions. The retail dealer adds a percentage to the wholesale prices, not, of course, always the same percentage, but still mostly the same. Given the wholesale price of most articles, you can commonly tell their retail price. Now wholesale transactions are commonly not cash transactions, but bill transactions. The duration of the bill varies with the custom of the trade; it may be two, three months, or six weeks, but there is always a bill. Times of credit mean times in which the bills of many people are taken readily; times of bad credit, times when the bills of much fewer people are taken, and even of those suspiciously. In times of good credit there are a great number of strong purchasers, and in times of bad credit only a smaller number of weak ones; and, therefore, years of improving credit, if there be no disturbing cause, are years of rising price, and years of decaying credit, years of falling price.

This is the meaning of the saying 'John Bull can stand many things, but he cannot stand two per cent:' it means that the greatest effect of the three great causes is nearly peculiar to England; here, and here almost alone, the excess of savings over investments is deposited in banks; here, and here only, is it made use of so as to affect trade at large; here, and here only, are prices gravely affected. In these circumstances, a low rate of interest, long protracted, is equivalent to a total depreciation of the precious metals. In his book on the effect of the great gold discoveries, Professor Jevons showed, and so far as I know, was the first to show, the necessity of eliminating these temporary

69

changes of value in gold before you could judge properly of the permanent depreciation. He proved, that in the years preceding both 1847 and 1857 there was a general rise of prices; and in the years succeeding these years, a great fall. The same might be shown of the years before and after 866, *mutatis mutandis.*

And at the present moment we have a still more remarkable example, which was thus analysed in the Economist of the 30th December, 1871, in an article which I venture to quote as a whole:

'THE GREAT RISE IN THE PRICE OF COMMODITIES.

'Most persons are aware that the trade of the country is in a state of great activity. All the usual tests indicate that--the state of the Revenue, the Bankers' Clearing-house figures, the returns of exports and imports are all plain, and all speak the same language. But few have, we think, considered one most remarkable feature of the present time, or have sufficiently examined its consequences. That feature is the great rise in the price of most of the leading articles of trade during the past year. We give at the foot of this paper a list of articles, comprising most first-rate articles of commerce, and it will be seen that the rise of price, though not universal and not uniform, is nevertheless very striking and very general. The most remarkable cases are--

		January			December		
		L,	s.	d.	L,	s.	d.
Wool--South Down hogs	per pack	13	0	0	21	15	0
Cotton--Upland ordinary	per lb.	0	0	7 1/4	0	0	8
No. 40 mule yarn, &c.	per lb.	0	1	1 1/2	0	1	2 1/2
Iron--Bars, British	per ton	7	2	6	8	17	6
Pig, No. 1 Clyde	per ton	2	13	3	3	16	0
Lead	per ton	18	7	6	8	17	6
Tin	per ton	137	0	0	157	0	0
Copper--Sheeting	per ton	75	10	0	95	0	0
Wheat (GAZETTE average)	per qr.	2	12	0	2	15	8

--and in other cases there is a tendency upwards in price much more often than there is a tendency downwards.

'This general rise of price must be due either to a diminution in the supply of the quoted articles, or to an increased demand for them. In some cases there has no doubt been a short supply. Thus in wool, the diminution in the home breed of sheep has had a great effect on the price--

In 1869 the home stock of sheep was 29,538,000
In 1871 27,133,000
Diminution 2,405,000
Equal to 8.1 per cent

and in the case of some other articles there may be a similar cause operating. But taking the whole mass of the supply of commodities in this country, as shown by the plain test of the quantities imported, it has not diminished, but augmented. The returns of the Board of Trade prove this in the most striking manner, and we give below a table of some of the important articles. The rise in prices must, therefore, be due to an increased demand, and the first question is, to what is that demand due?

'We believe it to be due to the combined operation of three causes cheap money, cheap corn, and improved credit. As to the first indeed, it might be said at first sight that so general an increase must be due to a depreciation of the precious metals. Certainly in many controversies facts far less striking have been alleged as proving it. And indeed there plainly is a diminution in the purchasing power of money, though that diminution is not general and permanent, but local and temporary. The peculiarity of the precious metals is that their value depends for unusually long periods on the quantity of them which is in the market. In the long run, their value, like that of all others, is determined by the cost at which they can be brought to market. But for all temporary purposes, it is the supply in the market which governs the price, and that supply in this country is exceedingly variable. After a commercial crisis, 1866 for example, two things happen: first, we call in the debts which are owing to us in foreign countries; and we require these debts to be paid to us, not in commodities, but in money. From this cause principally, and omitting minor causes, the bullion in the Bank of England, which was 13,156,000 L. in May 1866, rose to 19,413,000 L. in January 1867, being an increase of over 6,000,000 L. And then there comes also a second cause, tending in the same direction. During a depressed period the savings of the country increase considerably faster than the outlet for them. A person who has made savings does not know what to do with them. And this new unemployed saving means additional money. Till a saving is invested or employed it exists only in the form of money: a farmer who has sold his wheat and has 100 L. 'to the good,' holds that 100 L. in money, or some equivalent for money, till he sees some advantageous use to be made of it. Probably he places it in a bank, and this enables it to do more work. If 3,000,000 L. of coin be deposited in a bank, and it need only keep 1,000,000 L. as a reserve, that sets 2,000,000 L. free, and is for the time equivalent to an increase of so much coin. As a principle it may be laid down that all new unemployed savings require *either an increased stock of the precious metals, or an increase in the efficiency of the banking expedients by which these metals are economised.* In other words, in a saving and uninvesting period of the national industry, we accumulate gold, and augment the efficiency of our gold. If therefore such a saving period follows close upon an occasion when foreign credits have been diminished and foreign debts called in, the augmentation in the effective quantity of gold in the country is extremely great. The old money called in from abroad and the new money representing the new saving co-operate with one another. And their natural tendency is to cause a general rise in price, and what is the same thing, a diffused diminution in the purchasing power of money.

'Up to this point there is nothing special in the recent history of the money market. Similar events happened both after the panic of 1847, and after that of 1857. But there is another cause of the same kind, and acting in the same direction, which is peculiar to the present time; this cause is the amount of the foreign money, and especially of the money of foreign Governments, now in London. No Government probably ever had nearly as much at its command as the German Government now has. Speaking broadly, two things happened: during the war England was the best place of shelter for foreign money, and this made money more cheap here than it would otherwise have been; after the war England became the most convenient paying place, and the most convenient resting place for money, and this again has made money cheaper. The commercial causes, for which there are many precedents, have been aided by a political cause for the efficacy of which there is no precedent.

'But though plentiful money is necessary to high prices, and though it has a natural tendency to produce these prices, yet it is not of itself sufficient to produce them. In the cases we are dealing with, in order to lower prices there must not only be additional money, but a satisfactory mode of employing that additional money. This is obvious if we remember whence that augmented money is derived. It is derived from the savings of the people, and will only be invested in the manner which the holders for the time being consider suitable to such savings. It will not be used in mere expenditure; it would be contrary to the very nature of it so to use it. A new channel of demand is required to take off the new money, or that new money will not raise prices. It will lie idle in the banks, as we have often seen it. We should still see the frequent, the common phenomenon of dull trade and cheap money existing side by side.

'The demand in this case arose in the most effective of all ways. In 1867 and the first half of 1868 corn was dear, as the following figures show:

GAZETTE AVERAGE PRICE OF WHEAT.

		s.	d.
December,	1866	60	3
January,	1867	61	4
February		60	10
March		59	9
April		61	6
May		64	8
June		65	8
July		65	0
August		67	8
September		62	8
October	1867	66	6
November		69	5
December		67	4
January,	1868	70	3
February		73	0
March		73	0
April		73	3
May		73	9
June		67	11
July		65	5

From that time it fell, and it was very cheap during the whole of 1869 and 1870. The effect of this cheapness is great in every department of industry. The working classes, having cheaper food, need to spend so much less on that food, and have more to spend on other things. In consequence, there is a gentle augmentation of demand through almost all departments of trade. And this almost always causes a great augmentation in what may be called the instrumental trades--that is, in the trades which deal in machines and instruments used in many branches of commerce, and in the materials for such. Take, for instance, the iron trade--

```
In the year 1869 we exported 2,568,000 tons
 "        1870         "      2,716,000 tons
                                          5,284,000 tons
 "        1867         "      1,881,000 tons
 "        1868         "      1,944,000 tons
                                          3,826,000 tons
                              Increase    1,458,000 tons
```

that is to say, cheap corn operating throughout the world, created a new demand for many kinds of articles; the production of a large number of such articles being aided by iron in some one of its many forms, iron to that extent was exported. And the effect is cumulative. The manufacture of iron being stimulated, all persons concerned in that great manufacture are well off, have more to spend, and by spending it encourage other branches of manufacture, which again propagate the demand; they receive and so encourage industries in a third degree dependent and removed.

'It is quite true that corn has not been quite so cheap during the present year. But even if it had been dearer than it is, it would not all at once arrest the great trade which former cheapness had created. The "ball," if we may so say, "was set rolling" in 1869 and 1870, and a great increase of demand was then created in certain trades and propagated through all trades. A continuance of very high prices would produce the reverse effect; it would slacken demand in certain trades, and the effect would be gradually diffused through all trades. But a slight rise such as that of this year has no perceptible effect.

'When the stimulus of cheap corn is added to that of cheap money, the full conditions of a great and diffused rise of prices are satisfied. This new employment supplies a mode in which money can be invested. Bills are drawn of greater number and greater magnitude, and through the agencies of banks and discount houses, the savings of the country are invested in such bills. There is thus a new want and a new purchase-money to supply that want, and the consequence is the diffused and remarkable rise of price which the figures show to have occurred.

'The rise has also been aided by the revival of credit. This, as need not be at length explained, is a great aid to buying, and consequently a great aid to a rise of price. Since 1866, credit has been gradually, though very slowly, recovering, and it is probably as good as it is reasonable or proper that it should be. We are now trusting as many people as we ought to trust, and as yet there is no wild excess of misplaced confidence which would make us trust those whom we ought not to trust.'

The process thus explained is the common process. The surplus of loanable capital which lies in the hands of bankers is not employed by them in any original way; it is almost always lent to a trade already growing and already improving. The use of it develops that trade yet farther, and this again augments and stimulates other trades. Capital may long lie idle in a stagnant condition of industry; the mercantile securities which experienced bankers know to be good do not augment, and they will not invent other securities, or take bad ones.

In most great periods of expanding industry, the three great causes much loanable capital, good credit, and the increased profits derived from better-used labour and better-used capitalhave acted simultaneously; and though either may act by itself, there is a permanent reason why mostly they will act together. They both tend to grow together, if you begin from a period of depression. In such periods credit is bad, and industry unemployed; very generally provisions are high in price, and their dearness was one of the causes which made the times bad. Whether there was or was not too much loanable capital when that period begins, there soon comes to be too much. Quiet people continue to save part of their incomes in bad times as well as in good; indeed, of the two, people of slightly-varying and fixed incomes have better means of saving in bad times because prices are lower. Quiescent trade affords no new securities in which the new saving can be invested, and therefore there comes soon to be an excess of loanable capital. In a year or two after a crisis credit usually improves, as the remembrance of the disasters which at the crisis impaired credit is becoming fainter and fainter. Provisions get back to their usual price, or some great industry makes, from some temporary cause, a quick step forward. At these moments, therefore, the three agencies which, as has been explained, greatly develope trade, combine to develope it simultaneously.

The certain result is a bound of national prosperity; the country leaps forward as if by magic. But only part of that prosperity has a solid reason. As far as prosperity is based on a greater quantity of production, and that of the right articles as far as it is based on the increased rapidity with which commodities of every kind reach those who want them its basis is good. Human industry is more efficient, and therefore there is more to be divided among mankind. But in so far as that prosperity is based on a general rise of prices, it is only imaginary. A general rise of prices is a rise only in name; whatever anyone gains on the article which he has to sell he loses on the articles which he has to buy, and so he is just where he was. The only real effects of a general rise of prices are these: first, it straitens people of fixed incomes, who suffer as purchasers, but who have no gain to correspond; and secondly, it gives an extra profit to fixed capital created before the rise happened. Here the sellers gain, but without any equivalent loss as buyers. Thirdly, this gain on fixed capital is greatest in what may be called the industrial 'implements,' such as coal and iron. These are wanted in all industries, and in any general increase of prices, they are sure to rise much more than other things. Everybody wants them; the supply of them cannot be rapidly augmented, and therefore their price rises very quickly. But to the country as a whole, the general rise of prices is no benefit at all; it is simply a change of nomenclature for an identical relative value in the same commodities. Nevertheless, most people are happier for it; they think they are getting richer, though they are not. And as the rise does not happen on all articles at the same moment, but is propagated gradually through society, those to whom it first comes gain really; and as at first every one believes that he will gain when his own article is rising, a buoyant cheerfulness overflows the mercantile world.

This prosperity is precarious as far as it is real, and transitory in so far as it is fictitious. The augmented production, which is the reason of the real prosperity, depends on the full working of the whole industrial organisationof all capitalists and labourers; that prosperity was caused by that full working, and will cease with it. But that full working is liable to be destroyed by the occurrence of any great misfortune to any considerable industry. This would cause misfortune to the industries dependent on that one, and, as has been explained, all through society and back again. But every such industry is liable to grave fluctuations, and the most important--the provision industries--to the gravest and the suddenest. They are dependent on the casualties of the seasons. A single bad harvest diffused over the world, a succession of two or three bad harvests, even in England only, will raise the price of corn exceedingly, and will keep it high. And a great and protracted rise in the price of corn will at once destroy all the real part of the unusual prosperity of previous good times. It will change the full working of the industrial machine into an imperfect working; it will make the produce of that machine less than usual instead of more than usual; instead of there being more than the average of general dividend to be distributed between the producers, there will immediately be less than the average.

And in so far as the apparent prosperity is caused by an unusual plentifulness of loanable capital and a consequent rise in prices, that prosperity is not only liable to reaction, but certain to be exposed to reaction. The same causes which generate this prosperity will, after they have been acting a little longer, generate an equivalent adversity. The process is this: the plentifulness of loanable capital causes a rise of prices; that rise of prices makes it necessary to have more loanable capital to carry on the same trade. 100,000 L. will not buy as much when prices are high as it will when prices are low, it will not be so effectual for carrying on business; more money is necessary in dear times than in cheap times to produce the same changes in the same commodities. Even supposing trade to have remained stationary, a greater capital would be required to carry it on after such a rise of prices as has been described than was necessary before that rise. But in this case the trade will not have remained stationary; it will have increasedcertainly to some extent, probably to a great extent. The 'loanable capital,' the lending of which caused the rise of prices, was lent to enable it--to augment. The loanable capital lay idle in the banks till some trade started into prosperity, and then was lent in order to develope that trade; that trade caused other secondary developments; those secondary developments enabled more loanable capital to be lent; and that lending caused a tertiary development of trade; and so on through society.

In consequence, a long-continued low rate of interest is almost always followed by a rapid rise in that rate. Till the available trade is found it lies idle, and can scarcely be lent at all; some of it is not lent. But the moment the available trade is discoveredthe moment that prices have risen--the demand for loanable capital becomes keen. For the most part, men of business must carry on their regular trade; if it cannot be carried on without borrowing 10 per cent more capital, 10 per cent more capital they must borrow. Very often they have incurred obligations which must be met; and if that is so the rate of interest which they pay is comparatively indifferent. What is necessary to meet their acceptances they will borrow, pay for it what they may; they had better pay any price than permit those acceptances to be dishonoured. And in less extreme eases men of business have a fixed capital, which cannot lie idle except at a great loss; a set of labourers which must be, if possible, kept together; a steady connection of customers, which they would very unwillingly lose. To keep all these, they borrow; and in a period of high prices many merchants are peculiarly anxious to borrow, because the augmentation of the price of the article in which they deal makes them really see, or imagine that they see, peculiar opportunities of profit. An immense new borrowing soon follows upon the new and great trade, and the rate of interest rises at once, and generally rises rapidly.

This is the surer to happen that Lombard Street is, as has been shown before, a very delicate market. A large amount of money is held there by bankers and by bill-brokers at interest: this they must employ, or they will be ruined. It is better for them to reduce the rate they charge, and compensate themselves by reducing the rate they pay, rather than to keep up the rate of charge, if by so doing they cannot employ all their money. It is vital to them to employ all the money on which they pay interest. A little excess therefore forces down the rate of interest very much. But if that low rate of interest should cause, or should aid in causing, a great growth of trade, the rise is sure to be quick, and is apt to be violent. The figures of trade are reckoned by hundreds of millions, where those of loanable capital count only by millions. A great increase in the borrowing demands of English commerce almost always changes an excess of loanable capital above the demand to a greater deficiency below the demand. That deficiency causes adversity, or apparent adversity, in trade, just as, and in the same manner, that the previous excess caused prosperity, or apparent prosperity. It causes a fall of price that runs through society; that fall causes a decline of activity and a diminution of profitsa painful contraction instead of the previous pleasant expansion.

The change is generally quicker because some check to credit happens at an early stage of it. The mercantile community will have been unusually fortunate if during the period of rising prices it has not made great mistakes. Such a period naturally excites the sanguine and the ardent; they fancy that the prosperity they see will last always, that it is only the beginning of a greater prosperity. They altogether over-estimate the demand for the article they deal in, or the work they do. They all in their degreeand the ablest and the cleverest the mostwork much more than they should, and trade far above their means. Every great crisis reveals the excessive speculations of many houses which no one before suspected, and which commonly indeed had not begun or had not carried very far those speculations, till they were tempted by the daily rise of price and the surrounding fever.

The case is worse, because at most periods of great commercial excitement there is some mixture of the older and simpler kind of investing mania. Though the money of saving persons is in the hands of banks, and though, by offering interest, banks retain the command of much of it, yet they do not retain the command of the whole, or anything near the whole; all of it can be used, and much of it is used, by its owners. They speculate with it in bubble companies and in worthless shares, just as they did in the time of the South Sea mania, when there were no banks, and as they would again in England supposing that banks ceased to exist. The mania of 1825 and the mania of 1866 were striking examples of this; in their case to a great extent, as in most similar modern periods to a less extent, the delirium of ancient gambling co-operated with the milder madness of modern overtrading. At the very beginning of adversity, the counters in the gambling mama, the shares in the companies created to feed the mania, are discovered to be worthless; down they all go, and with them much of credit.

The good times too of high price almost always engender much fraud. All people are most credulous when they are most happy; and when much money has just been made, when some people are really making it, when most people think they are making it, there is a happy opportunity for ingenious mendacity. Almost everything will be believed for a little while, and long before discovery the worst and most adroit deceivers are geographically or legally beyond the reach of punishment. But the harm they have done diffuses harm, for it weakens credit still farther.

When we understand that Lombard Street is subject to severe alternations of opposite causes, we should cease to be surprised at its seeming cycles. We should cease too to be surprised at the sudden panics. During the period of reaction and adversity, just even at the last instant of prosperity, the whole structure is delicate. The peculiar essence of our banking system is an unprecedented trust between man and man: and when that trust is much weakened by hidden causes, a small accident may greatly hurt it, and a great accident for a moment may almost destroy it.

Now too that we comprehend the inevitable vicissitudes of Lombard Street, we can also thoroughly comprehend the cardinal importance of always retaining a great banking reserve. Whether the times of adversity are well met or ill met depends far more on this than on any other single circumstance. If the reserve be large, its magnitude sustains credit; and if it be small, its diminution stimulates the gravest apprehensions. And the better we comprehend the importance of the banking reserve, the higher we shall estimate the responsibility of those who keep it.

CHAPTER VII.

A More Exact Account of the Mode in Which the Bank of England
Has Discharged Its Duty of Retaining a Good Bank Reserve,
and of Administering It Effectually.

The preceding chapters have in some degree enabled us to appreciate the importance of the duties which the Bank of England is bound to discharge as to its banking reserve.

If we ask how the Bank of England has discharged this great responsibility, we shall be struck by three things: first, as has been said before, the Bank has never by any corporate act or authorised utterance acknowledged the duty, and some of its directors deny it; second (what is even more remarkable), no resolution of Parliament, no report of any Committee of Parliament (as far as I know), no remembered speech of a responsible statesman, has assigned or enforced that duty on the Bank; third (what is more remarkable still), the distinct teaching of our highest authorities has often been that no public duty of any kind is imposed on the Banking Department of the Bank; that, for banking purposes, it is only a joint stock bank like any other bank; that its managers should look only to the interest of the proprietors and their dividend; that they are to manage as the London and Westminster Bank or the Union Bank manages.

At first, it seems exceedingly strange that so important a responsibility should be unimposed, unacknowledged, and denied; but the explanation is this. We are living amid the vestiges of old controversies, and we speak their language, though we are dealing with different thoughts and different facts. For more than fifty yearsfrom 1793 down to 1844, there was a keen controversy as to the public duties of the Bank. It was said to be the 'manager' of the paper currency, and on that account many expected much good from it; others said it did great harm; others again that it could do neither good nor harm. But for the whole period there was an incessant and fierce discussion. That discussion was terminated by the Act of 1844. By that Act the currency manages itself; the entire working is automatic. The Bank of England plainly does not manage--cannot even be said to manage--the currency any more. And naturally, but rashly, the only reason upon which a public responsibility used to be assigned to the

Bank having now clearly come to an end, it was inferred by many that the Bank had no responsibility. The complete uncertainty as to the degree of responsibility acknowledged by the Bank of England is best illustrated by what has been said by the Bank directors themselves as to the panic of 1866. The panic of that year, it will be remembered, happened, contrary to precedent, in the spring, and at the next meeting of the Court of Bank proprietors--the September meeting--there was a very remarkable discussion, which I give at length below, and of which all that is most material was thus described in the 'Economist':

'THE GREAT IMPORTANCE OF THE LATE MEETING OF THE PROPRIETORS OF THE BANK OF ENGLAND.

'The late meeting of the proprietors of the Bank of England has a very unusual importance. There can be no effectual inquiry now into the history of the late crisis. A Parliamentary committee next year would, unless something strange occur in the interval, be a great waste of time. Men of business have keen sensations but short memories, and they will care no more next February for the events of last May than they now care for the events of October 1864. A pro forma inquiry, on which no real mind is spent, and which everyone knows will lead to nothing, is far worse than no inquiry at all. Under these circumstances the official statements of the Governor of the Bank are the only authentic expositions we shall have of the policy of the Bank Directors, whether as respects the past or the future. And when we examine the proceedings with care, we shall find that they contain matter of the gravest import.

'This meeting may be considered to admit and recognise the fact that the Bank of England keeps the sole banking reserve of the country. We do not now mix up this matter with the country circulation, or the question whether there should be many issuers of notes or only one. We speak not of the currency reserve, but of the banking reserve--the reserve held against deposits, and not the reserve held against notes. We have often insisted in these columns that the Bank of England does keep the sole real reserve--the sole considerable unoccupied mass of cash in the country; but there has been no universal agreement about it. Great authorities have been unwilling to admit it. They have not, indeed, formally and explicitly contended against it. If they had, they must have pointed out some other great store of unused cash besides that at the Bank, and they could not find such store. But they have attempted distinctions; have said that the doctrine that the Bank of England keeps the sole banking reserve of the country was "not a good way of putting it," was exaggerated, and was calculated to mislead.

'But the late meeting is a complete admission that such is the fact. The Governor of the Bank said:

"'A great strain has within the last few months been put upon the resources of this house, and of the whole banking community of London; and I think I am entitled to say that not only this house, but the entire banking body, acquitted themselves most honourably and creditably throughout that very trying period. Banking is a very peculiar business, and it depends so much upon credit that the least blast of suspicion is sufficient to sweep away, as it were, the harvest of a whole year. But the manner in which the banking establishments generally in London met the demands made upon them during the greater portion of the past half-year affords a most satisfactory proof of the soundness of the principles on which their business is conducted. This house exerted itself to the utmostand exerted itself most successfully--to meet the crisis. We did not flinch from our post. When the storm came upon us, on the morning on which it became known that the house of Overend and Co. had failed, we were in as sound and healthy a position as any banking establishment could hold, and on that day and throughout the succeeding week we made advances which would hardly be credited. I do not believe that anyone would have thought of predicting, even at the shortest period beforehand, the greatness of those advances. It was not unnatural that in this state of things a certain degree of alarm should have taken possession of the public mind, and that those who required accommodation from the Bank should have gone to the Chancellor of the Exchequer and requested the Government to empower us to issue notes beyond the statutory amount, if we should think that such a measure was desirable. But we had to act before we could receive any such power, and before the Chancellor of the Exchequer was perhaps out of his bed we had advanced one-half of our reserves, which were certainly thus reduced to an amount which we could not witness without regret. But we would not flinch from the duty which we conceived was imposed upon us of supporting the banking community, and I am not aware that any legitimate application made for assistance to this house was refused. Every gentleman who came here with adequate security was liberally dealt with, and if accommodation could not be afforded to the full extent which was demanded, no one who offered proper security failed to obtain relief from this house."

'Now this is distinctly saying that the other banks of the country need not keep any such banking reserveany such sum of actual cashof real sovereigns and bank notes, as will help them through a sudden panic. It acknowledges a "duty" on the part of the Bank of England to "support the banking community," to make the reserve of the Bank of England do for them as well as for itself.

'In our judgment this language is most just, and the Governor of the Bank could scarcely have done a greater public service than by using language so businesslike and so distinct. Let us know precisely who is to keep the banking reserve. If the joint stock banks and the private banks and the country banks are to keep their share, let us determine on that; Mr. Gladstone appeared not long since to say in Parliament that it ought to be so. But at any rate there should be no doubt whose duty it is. Upon grounds which we have often stated, we believe that the anomaly of one bank keeping the sole banking reserve is so fixed in our system that we cannot change it if we would. The great evil to be feared was an indistinct conception of the fact, and that is now avoided.

'The importance of these declarations by the Bank is greater, because after the panic of 1857 the bank did not hold exactly the same language. A person who loves concise expressions said lately "that Overends broke the Bank in 1866 because it went, and in 1857 because it was not let go." We need not too precisely examine such language; the element of truth in it is very plain--the great advances made to Overends were a principal event in the panic of 1857; the bill-brokers were then very much what the bankers were lately they were the borrowers who wanted sudden and incalculable advances. But the bill-brokers were told not to expect the like again. But Alderman Salomons, on the part of the London bankers, said, "he wished to take that opportunity of stating that he believed nothing could be more satisfactory to the managers and shareholders of joint stock banks than the testimony which the Governor of the Bank of England had that day borne to the sound and honourable manner in which their business was conducted. It was manifestly desirable that the joint stock banks and the banking interest generally should work in harmony with the Bank of England; and he sincerely thanked the Governor of the Bank for the kindly manner in which he had alluded to the mode in which the joint stock banks had met the late monetary crisis." The Bank of England agrees to give other banks the requisite assistance in case of need, and the other banks agree to ask for it.

'Secondly. The Bank agrees, in fact, if not in name, to make limited advances on proper security to anyone who applies for it. On the present occasion 45,000,000 L. was so advanced in three months. And the Bank do not say to the mercantile community, or to the bankers, "Do not come to us again. We helped you once. But do not look upon it as a precedent. We will not help you again." On the contrary, the evident and intended implication is that under like circumstances the Bank would act again as it has now acted.'

This article was much disliked by many of the Bank directors, and especially by some whose opinion is of great authority. They thought that the 'Economist' drew 'rash deductions' from a speech which was in itself 'open to some objection'which was, like all such speeches, defective in theoretical precision, and which was at best only the expression of an opinion by the Governor of that day, which had not been authorised by the Court of Directors, which could not bind the Bank. However the article had at least this use, that it brought out the facts. All the directors would have felt a difficulty in commenting upon, or limiting, or in differing from, a speech of a Governor from the chair. But there was no difficulty or delicacy in attacking the 'Economist.' Accordingly Mr. Hankey, one of the most experienced bank directors, not long after, took occasion to observe: 'The "Economist" newspaper has put forth what in my opinion is the most mischievous doctrine ever broached in the monetary or banking world in this country; viz, that it is the proper function of the Bank of England to keep money available at all times to supply the demands of bankers who have rendered their own assets unavailable. Until such a doctrine is repudiated by the banking interest, the difficulty of pursuing any sound principle of banking in London will be always very great. But I do not believe that such a doctrine as that bankers are justified in relying on the Bank of England to assist them in time of need is generally held by the bankers in London.

'I consider it to be the undoubted duty of the Bank of England to hold its banking deposits (reserving generally about one-third in cash) in the most available securities; and in the event of a sudden pressure in the money market, by whatever circumstance it may be caused, to bear its full share of a drain on its resources. I am ready to admit, however, that a general opinion has long prevailed that the Bank of England ought to be prepared to do much more than this, though I confess my surprise at finding an advocate for such an opinion in the "Economist." If it were practicable for the Bank to retain money unemployed to meet such an emergency, it would be a very unwise thing to do so. But I contend that it is quite impracticable, and if it were possible, it would be most inexpedient; and I can only express my regret that the Bank, from a desire to do everything in its power to afford general assistance in times of banking or commercial distress, should ever have acted in a way to encourage such an opinion. The more the conduct of the affairs of the Bank is made to assimilate to the conduct of every other well-managed bank in the United Kingdom, the better for the Bank, and the better for the community at large.'

I am scarcely a judge, but I do not think Mr. Hankey replies to the 'Economist' very conclusively.

First. He should have observed that the question is not as to what 'ought to be,' but as to what is. The 'Economist' did not say that the system of a single bank reserve was a good system, but that it was the system which existed, and which must be worked, as you could not change it.

Secondly. Mr. Hankey should have shown 'some other store of unused cash' except the reserve in the Banking Department of the Bank of England out of which advances in time of panic could be made. These advances are necessary, and must be made by someone. The 'reserves' of London bankers are not such store; they are used cash, not unused; they are part of the Bank deposits, and lent as such.

Thirdly. Mr. Hankey should have observed that we know by the published figures that the joint stock banks of London do not keep one-third, or anything like one-third, of their liabilities in 'cash' even meaning by 'cash' a deposit at the Bank of England. One-third of the deposits in joint stock banks, not to speak of the private banks, would be 30,000,000 L.; and the private deposits of the Bank of England are

18,000,000 L. According to his own statement, there is a conspicuous contrast. The joint stock banks, and the private banks, no doubt, too, keep one sort of reserve, and the Bank of England a different kind of reserve altogether. Mr. Hankey says that the two ought to be managed on the same principle; but if so, he should have said whether he would assimilate the practice of the Bank of England to that of the other banks, or that of the other banks to the practice of the Bank of England.

Fourthly. Mr. Hankey should have observed that, as has been explained, in most panics, the principal use of a 'banking reserve' is not to advance to bankers; the largest amount is almost always advanced to the mercantile public and to bill-brokers. But the point is, that by our system all extra pressure is thrown upon the Bank of England. In the worst part of the crisis of 1866, 50,000 L. 'fresh money' could not be borrowed, even on the best securityeven on Consols except at the Bank of England. There was no other lender to new borrowers.

But my object now is not to revive a past controversy, but to show in what an unsatisfactory and uncertain condition that controversy has left a most important subject. Mr. Hankey's is the last explanation we have had of the policy of the Bank. He is a very experienced and attentive director, and I think expresses, more or less, the opinions of other directors. And what do we find? Setting aside and saying nothing about the remarkable speech of the Governor in 1866, which at least (according to the interpretation of the 'Economist') was clear and excellent, Mr. Hankey leaves us in doubt altogether as to what will be the policy of the Bank of England in the next panic, and as to what amount of aid the public may then expect from it. His words are too vague. No one can tell what a 'fair share' means; still less can we tell what other people at some future time will say it means. Theory suggests, and experience proves, that in a panic the holders of the ultimate Bank reserve (whether one bank or many) should lend to all that bring good securities quickly, freely, and readily. By that policy they allay a panic; by every other policy they intensify it. The public have a right to know whether the Bank of Englandthe holders of our ultimate bank reserveacknowledge this duty, and are ready to perform it. But this is now very uncertain.

If we refer to history, and examine what in fact has been the conduct of the Bank directors, we find that they have acted exactly as persons of their type, character, and position might have been expected to act. They are a board of plain, sensible, prosperous English merchants; and they have both done and left undone what such a board might have been expected to do and not to do. Nobody could expect great attainments in economical science from such a board; laborious study is for the most part foreign to the habits of English merchants. Nor could we expect original views on banking, for banking is a special trade, and English merchants, as a body, have had no experience in it. A 'board' can scarcely ever make improvements, for the policy of a board is determined by the opinions of the most numerous class of its membersits average membersand these are never prepared for sudden improvements. A board of upright and sensible merchants will always act according to what it considers 'safe' principles--that is, according to the received maxims of the mercantile world then and thereand in this manner the directors of the Bank of England have acted nearly uniformly. Their strength and their weakness were curiously exemplified at the time when they had the most power. After the suspension of cash payments in 1797, the directors of the Bank of England could issue what notes they liked. There was no check; these notes could not come back upon the Bank for payment; there was a great temptation to extravagant issue, and no present penalty upon it. But the directors of the Bank withstood the temptation; they did not issue their inconvertible notes extravagantly. And the proof is, that for more than ten years after the suspension of cash payments the Bank paper was undepreciated, and circulated at no discount in comparison with gold. Though the Bank directors of that day at last fell into errors, yet on the whole they acted with singular judgment and moderation. But when, in 1810, they came to be examined as to their reasons, they gave answers that have become almost classical by their nonsense. Mr. Pearse, the Governor of the Bank, said: 'In considering this subject, with reference to the manner in which bank-notes are issued, resulting from the applications made for discounts to supply the necessary want of bank-notes, by which their issue in amount is so controlled that it can never amount to an excess, I cannot see how the amount of bank-notes issued can operate upon the price of bullion, or the state of the exchanges; and therefore I am individually of opinion that the price of bullion, or the state of the exchanges, can never be a reason for lessening the amount of banknotes to be issued, always understanding the control which I have already described.

'Is the Governor of the Bank of the same opinion which has now been expressed by the Deputy-Governor?

'Mr. Whitmore, I am so much of the same opinion, that I never think it necessary to advert to the price of gold, or the state of the exchange, on the days on which we make our advances.

'Do you advert to these two circumstances with a view to regulate the general amount of your advances?--I do not advert to it with a view to our general advances, conceiving it not to bear upon the question.

And Mr. Harman, another Bank director, expressed his opinion in these terms: 'I must very materially alter my opinions before I can suppose that the exchanges will be influenced by any modifications of our paper currency.'

Very few persons perhaps could have managed to commit so many blunders in so few words.

But it is no disgrace at all to the Bank directors of that day to have committed these blunders. They spoke according to the best mercantile opinion of England. The City of London and the House of Commons both approved of what they said; those who dissented were said to be abstract thinkers and unpractical men. The Bank directors adopted the ordinary opinions, and pursued the usual practice of their time. It was this 'routine' that caused their moderation. They believed that so long as they issued 'notes' only at 5 per cent, and only on the discount of good bills, those notes could not be depreciated. And as the number of 'good' billsbills which sound merchants know to be gooddoes not rapidiy increase, and as the market rate of interest was often less than 5 per cent, these checks on over-issue were very effective. They failed in time, and the theory upon which they were defended was nonsense; but for a time their operation was powerful and excellent.

Unluckily, in the management of the matter before us--the management of the Bank reserve--the directors of the Bank of England were neither acquainted with right principles, nor were they protected by a judicious routine. They could not be expected themselves to discover such principles. The abstract thinking of the world is never to be expected from persons in high places; the administration of first-rate current transactions is a most engrossing business, and those charged with them are usually but little inclined to think on points of theory, even when such thinking most nearly concerns those transactions. No doubt when men's own fortunes are at stake, the instinct of the trader does somehow anticipate the conclusions of the closet. But a board has no instincts when it is not getting an income for its members, and when it is only discharging a duty of office. During the suspension of cash paymentsa suspension which lasted twenty-two yearsall traditions as to a cash reserve had died away. After 1819 the Bank directors had to discharge the duty of keeping a banking reserve, and (as the law then stood) a currency reserve also, without the guidance either of keen interests, or good principles, or wise traditions.

Under such circumstances, the Bank directors inevitably made mistakes of the gravest magnitude. The first time of trial came in 1825. In that year the Bank directors allowed their stock of bullion to fall in the most alarming manner:

On Dec. 24, 1824, the coin and bullion in the Bank was L10,721,000

On Dec. 25, 1825, it was reduced to L1,260,000

and the consequence was a panic so tremendous that its results are well remembered after nearly fifty years. In the next period of extreme trialin 1837, the Bank was compelled to draw for 2,000,000 L. on the Bank of France; and even after that aid the directors permitted their bullion, which was still the currency reserve as well as the banking reserve, to be reduced to 2,404,000 L.: a great alarm pervaded society, and generated an eager controversy, out of which ultimately emerged the Act of 1844. The next trial came in 1847, and then the Bank permitted its banking reserve (which the law had now distinctly separated) to fall to 1,176,000 L.; and so intense was the alarm, that the executive Government issued a letter of licence, permitting the Bank, if necessary, to break the new law, and, if necessary, to borrow from the currency reserve, which was full, in aid of the banking reserve, which was empty. Till 1857 there was an unusual calm in the money market, but in the autumn of that year the Bank directors let the banking reserve, which even in October was far too small, fall thus:

Oct. 10 4,024,000 L
Oct. 17 3,217,000 L
Oct. 24 3,485,000 L
Oct. 31 2,258,000 L

Nov. 6 2,155,000 L
Nov. 13   957,000 L

And then a letter of licence like that of 1847 was not only issued, but used. The Ministry of the day authorised the Bank to borrow from the currency reserve in aid of the banking reserve, and the Bank of England did so borrow several hundred pounds till the end of the month of November. A more miserable catalogue than that of the failures of the Bank of England to keep a good banking reserve in all the seasons of trouble between 1825 and 1857 is scarcely to be found in history.

But since 1857 there has been a great improvement. By painful events and incessant discussions, men of business have now been trained to see that a large banking reserve is necessary, and to understand that, in the curious constitution of the English banking world, the Bank of England is the only body which could effectually keep it. They have never acknowledged the duty; some of them, as we have seen, deny the duty; still they have to a considerable extent begun to perform the duty. The Bank directors, being experienced and able men of business, comprehended this like other men of business. Since 1857 they have always kept, I do not say a sufficient banking reserve, but a fair and creditable banking reserve, and one altogether different from any which they kept before. At one period the Bank directors even went farther: they made a distinct step in advance of the public intelligence; they adopted a particular mode of raising the rate of interest, which is far more efficient than any other mode. Mr. Goschen observes, in his book on the Exchanges: 'Between the rates in London and Paris, the expense of sending gold to and fro having been reduced to a minimum between the two cities, the difference can never be very great; but it must not be forgotten that, the interest being taken at a percentage calculated per annum, and the probable profit having, when an operation in three-month bills is contemplated, to be divided by four, whereas the percentage of expense has to be wholly borne by the one transaction, a very slight expense becomes a great impediment. If the cost is only 1/2 per cent, there must be a profit of 2 per cent in the rate of interest, or 1/2 per cent on three months, before any advantage commences; and thus, supposing that Paris capitalists calculate that they may send their gold over to England for 1/2 per cent expense, and chance their being so favoured by the Exchanges as to be able to draw it back without any cost at all, there must nevertheless be an excess of more than 2 per cent in the London rate of interest over that in Paris, before the operation of sending gold over from France, merely for the sake of the higher interest, will pay.'

Accordingly, Mr. Goschen recommended that the Bank of England should, as a rule, raise their rate by steps of 1 per cent at a time when the object of the rise was to affect the 'foreign Exchanges.' And the Bank of England, from 1860 onward, have acted upon that principle. Before that time they used to raise their rate almost always by steps of 1/2 per cent, and there was nothing in the general state of mercantile opinion to compel them to change their policy. The change was, on the contrary, most unpopular. On this occasion, and, as far as I know, on this occasion alone, the Bank of England made an excellent alteration of their policy, which was not exacted by contemporary opinion, and which was in advance of it. The beneficial results of the improved policy of the Bank were palpable and speedy. We were enabled by it to sustain the great drain of silver from Europe to India to pay for Indian cotton in the years between 18621865. In the autumn of 1864 there was especial danger; but, by a rapid and able use of their new policy, the Bank of England maintained an adequate reserve, and preserved the country from calamities which, if we had looked only to precedent, would have seemed inevitable. All the causes which produced the panic of 1857 were in action in 1864the drain of silver in 1864 and the preceding year was beyond comparison greater than in 1857 and the years before itand yet in 1864 there was no panic. The Bank of England was almost immediately rewarded for its adoption of right principles by finding that those principles, at a severe crisis, preserved public credit.

In 1866 undoubtedly a panic occurred, but I do not think that the Bank of England can be blamed for it. They had in their till an exceedingly good reserve according to the estimate of that timea sufficient reserve, in all probability, to have coped with the crises of 1847 and 1857. The suspension of Overend and Gurneythe most trusted private firm in Englandcaused an alarm, in suddenness and magnitude, without example. What was the effect of the Act of 1844 on the panic of 1866 is a question on which opinion will be long divided; but I think it will be generally agreed that, acting under the provisions of that law, the directors of the Bank of England had in their banking department in that year a fairly large reserve quite as large a reserve as anyone expected them to keepto meet unexpected and painful contingencies.

From 1866 to 1870 there was almost an unbroken calm on the money market. The Bank of England had no difficulties to cope with; there was no opportunity for much discretion. The money market took care of itself. But in 1870 the Bank of France suspended specie payments, and from that time a new era begins. The demands on this market for bullion have been greater, and have been more incessant, than they ever were before, for this is now the only bullion market. This has made it necessary for the Bank of England to hold a much larger banking reserve than was ever before required, and to be much more watchful than in former times lest that banking reserve should on a sudden be dangerously diminished. The forces are greater and quicker than they used to be, and a firmer protection and a surer solicitude are necessary. But I do not think the Bank of England is sufficiently aware of this. All the governing body of the Bank certainly are not aware of it. The same eminent director to whom I have before referred, Mr. Hankey, published in the 'Times' an elaborate letter, saying again that one-third of the liabilities were, even in these altered times, a sufficient reserve for the Banking Department of the Bank of England, and that it was no part of the business of the Bank to keep a supply of 'bullion for exportation,' which was exactly the most mischievous doctrine that could be maintained when the Banking Department of the Bank of England had become the only great repository in Europe where gold could at once be obtained, and when, therefore, a far greater store of bullion ought to be kept than at any former period.

And besides this defect of the present time, there are some chronic faults in the policy of the Bank of England, which arise, as will be presently explained, from grave defects in its form of government.

There is almost always some hesitation when a Governor begins to reign. He is the Prime Minister of the Bank Cabinet; and when so important a functionary changes, naturally much else changes too. If the Governor be weak, this kind of vacillation and hesitation continues throughout his term of office. The usual defect then is, that the Bank of England does not raise the rate of interest sufficiently quickly. It does raise it; in the end it takes the alarm, but it does not take the alarm sufficiently soon. A cautious man, in a new office, does not like strong measures. Bank Governors are generally cautious men; they are taken from a most cautious class; in consequence they are very apt to temporise and delay. But almost always the delay in creating a stringency only makes a greater stringency inevitable. The effect of a timid policy has been to let the gold out of the Bank, and that gold must be recovered. It would really have been far easier to have maintained the reserve by timely measures than to have replenished it by delayed measures; but new Governors rarely see this.

Secondly. Those defects are apt, in part, or as a whole, to be continued throughout the reign of a weak Governor. The objection to a decided policy, and the indisposition to a timely action, which are excusable in one whose influence is beginning, and whose reign is new, is continued through the whole reign of one to whom those defects are natural, and who exhibits those defects in all his affairs.

Thirdly. This defect is enhanced, because, as has so often been said, there is now no adequate rule recognised in the management of the banking reserve. Mr. Weguelin, the last Bank Governor who has been examined, said that it was sufficient for the Bank to keep from one-fourth to one-third of its banking liabilities as a reserve. But no one now would ever be content if the banking reserve were near to one-fourth of its liabilities. Mr. Hankey, as I have shown, considers 'about a third' as the proportion of reserve to liability at which the Bank should aim; but he does not say whether he regards a third as the minimum below which the reserve in the Banking Department should never be, or as a fair average, about which the reserve may fluctuate, sometimes being greater, or at others less.

In a future chapter I shall endeavour to show that one-third of its banking liabilities is at present by no means an adequate reserve for the Banking Departmentthat it is not even a proper minimum, far less a fair average; and I shall allege what seem to me good reasons for thinking that, unless the Bank aim by a different method at a higher standard, its own position may hereafter be perilous, and the public may be exposed to disaster.

II.

But, as has been explained, the Bank of England is bound, according to our system, not only to keep a good reserve against a time of panic, but to use that reserve effectually when that time of panic comes. The keepers of the Banking reserve, whether one or many, are obliged then to use that reserve for their own safety. If they permit all other forms of credit to perish, their own will perish immediately, and in consequence.

As to the Bank of England, however, this is denied. It is alleged that the Bank of England can keep aloof in a panic; that it can, if it will, let other banks and trades fail; that if it chooses, it can stand alone, and survive intact while all else perishes around it. On various occasions, most influential persons, both in the government of the Bank and out of it, have said that such was their opinion. And we must at once see whether this opinion is true or false, for it is absurd to attempt to estimate the conduct of the Bank of England during panics before we know what the precise position of the Bank in a panic really is.

The holders of this opinion in its most extreme form say, that in a panic the Bank of England can stay its hand at any time; that, though it has advanced much, it may refuse to advance more; that though the reserve may have been reduced by such advances, it may refuse to lessen it still further; that it can refuse to make any further dis counts; that the bills which it has discounted will become due; that it can refill its reserve by the payment of those bills; that it can sell stock or other securities, and so replenish its reserve still further. But in this form the notion scarcely merits serious refutation. If the Bank reserve has once become low, there are, in a panic, no means of raising it again. Money parted with at such a time is very hard to get back; those who have taken it will not let it gonot, at least, unless they are sure of getting other money in its place. And at such instant the recovery of money is as hard for the Bank of England as for any one else, probably even harder. The difficulty is this: if the Bank decline to discount, the holders of the bills previously discounted cannot pay. As has been shown, trade in England is largely carried on with borrowed money. If you propose greatly to reduce that amount, you will cause many failures unless you can pour in from elsewhere some equivalent amount of new money. But in a panic there is no new money to be had; everybody who has it clings to it, and will not part with it. Especially what has been advanced to merchants cannot easily be recovered; they are under immense liabilities, and they will not give back a penny which they imagine that even possibly they may need to discharge those liabilities. And bankers are in even greater terror. In a panic they will not discount a host of new bills; they are engrossed with their own liabilities and those of their own customers, and do not care for those of others. The notion that the Bank of England can stop discounting in a panic, and so obtain fresh money, is a delusion. It can stop discounting, of course, at pleasure. But if it does, it will get in no new money; its bill case will daily be more and more packed with bills 'returned unpaid.'

The sale of stock, too, by the Bank of England in the middle of a panic is impossible. The bank at such a time is the only lender on stock, and it is only by loans from a bank that large purchases, at such a moment, can be made. Unless the Bank of England lend, no stock will be bought. There is not in the country any large sum of unused ready money ready to buy it. The only unused sum is the reserve in the Banking Department of the Bank of England: if, therefore, in a panic that Department itself attempt to sell stock, the failure would be ridiculous. It would hardly be able to sell any at all. Probably it would not sell fifty pounds' worth. The idea that the Bank can, during a panic, replenish its reserve in this or in any other manner when that reserve has once been allowed to become empty, or nearly empty, is too absurd to be steadily maintained, though I fear that it is not yet wholly abandoned.

The second and more reasonable conception of the independence of the Bank of England is, however, this: It may be said, and it is said, that if the Bank of England stop at the beginning of a panic, if it refuse to advance a shilling more than usual, if it begin the battle with a good banking reserve, and do not diminish it by extra loans, the Bank of England is sure to be safe. But this form of the opinion, though more reasonable and moderate, is not, therefore, more true. The panic of 1866 is the best instance to test it. As everyone knows, that panic began quite suddenly, on the fall of 'Overends.' Just before, the Bank had 5,812,000 L. in its reserve; in fact, it advanced 13,000,000 L. of new money in the next few days, and its reserve went down to nothing, and the Government had to help. But if the Bank had not made these advances, could it have kept its reserve?

Certainly it could not. It could not have retained its own deposits. A large part of these are the deposits of bankers, and they would not consent to help the Bank of England in a policy of isolation. They would not agree to suspend payments themselves, and permit the Bank of England to survive, and get all their business. They would withdraw their deposits from the Bank; they would not assist it to stand erect amid their ruin. But even if this were not so, even if the banks were willing to keep their deposits at the Bank while it was not lending, they would soon find that they could not do it. They are only able to keep those deposits at the Bank by the aid of the Clearing-house system, and if a panic were to pass a certain height, that system, which rests on confidence, would be destroyed by terror.

The common course of business is this. A B having to receive 50,000 l. from C D takes C D's cheque on a banker crossed, as it is called, and, therefore, only payable to another banker. He pays that cheque to his own credit with his own banker, who presents it to the banker on whom it is drawn, and if good it is an item between them in the general clearing or settlement of the afternoon. But this is evidently a very refined machinery, which a panic will be apt to destroy. At the first stage A B may say to his debtor C D, 'I cannot take your cheque, I must have bank-notes.' If it is a debt on securities, he will be very apt to say this. The usual practicecredit being goodis for the creditor to take the debtor's cheque, and to give up the securities. But if the 'securities' really secure him in a time of difficulty, he will not like to give them up, and take a bit of paper a mere cheque, which may be paid or not paid. He will say to his debtor, 'I can only give you your securities if you will give me banknotes.' And if he does say so, the debtor must go to his bank, and draw out the 50,000 L. if he has it. But if this were done on a large scale, the bank's 'cash in house' would soon be gone; as the Clearing-house was gradually superseded it would have to trench on its deposit at the Bank of England; and then the bankers would have to pay so much over the counter that they would be unable to keep much money at the Bank, even if they wished. They would soon be obliged to draw out every shilling.

The diminished use of the Clearing-house, in consequence of the panic, would intensify that panic. By far the greater part of the bargains of the country in moneyed securities is settled on the Stock Exchange twice a month, and the number of securities then given up for mere cheques, and the number of cheques then passing at the Clearing-house are enormous. If that system collapse, the number of failures would be incalculable, and each failure would add to the discredit that caused the collapse.

The non-banking customers of the Bank of England would be discredited as well as other people; their cheques would not be taken any more than those of others; they would have to draw out banknotes, and the Bank reserve would not be enough for a tithe of such payments.

The matter would come shortly to this: a great number of brokers and dealers are under obligations to pay immense sums, and in common times they obtain these sums by the transfer of certain securities. If, as we said just now, No. 1 has borrowed 50,000 L. of No. 2 on Exchequer bills, he, for the most part, cannot pay No. 2 till he has sold or pledged those bills to some one else. But till he has the bills he cannot pledge or sell them; and if No. 2 will not give them up till he gets his money, No. 1 will be ruined, because he caunot pay it. And if No. 2 has No. 3 to pay, as is very likely, he may be ruined because of No. 1's default, and No. 4 only on account of No. 3's default; and so on without end. On settling day, without the Clearing-house, there would be a mass of failures, and a bundle of securities. The effect of these failures would be a general run on all bankers, and on the Bank of England particularly.

It may indeed be said that the money thus taken from the Banking Department of the Bank of England would return there immediately; that the public who borrowed it would not know where else to deposit it; that it would be taken out in the morning, and put back in the evening. But, in the first place, this argument assumes that the Banking Department would have enough money to pay the demands on it; and this is a mistake: the Banking Department would not have a hundredth part of the necessary funds. And in the second, a great panic which deranged the Clearing-house would soon be diffused all through the country. The money therefore taken from the Bank of England could not be soon returned to the Bank; it would not come back on the evening of the day on which it was taken out, or for many days; it would be distributed through the length and breadth of the country, wherever there were bankers, wherever there was trade, wherever there were liabilities, wherever there was terror.

And even in London, so immense a panic would soon impair the credit of the Banking Department of the Bank of England. That department has no great prestige. It was only created in 1844, and it has failed three times since. The world would imagine that what has happened before will happen again; and when they have got money, they will not deposit it at an establishment which may not be able to repay it. This did not happen in former panics, because the case we are considering never arose. The Bank was helping the public, and, more or less confidently, it was believed that the Government would help the Bank. But if the policy be relinquished which formerly assuaged alarm, that alarm will be protracted and enhanced, till it touch the Banking Department of the Bank itself.

I do not imagine that it would touch the Issue Department. I think that the public would be quite satisfied if they obtained banknotes. Generally nothing is gained by holding the notes of a bank instead of depositing them at a bank. But in the Bank of England there is a great difference: their notes are legal tender. Whoever holds them can always pay his debts, and, except for foreign payments, he could want no more. The rush would be for bank-notes; those that could be obtained would be carried north, south, east, and west, and, as there would not be enough for all the country, the Banking Department would soon pay away all it had.

Nothing, therefore, can be more certain than that the Bank of England has in this respect no peculiar privilege; that it is simply in the position of a Bank keeping the Banking reserve of the country; that it must in time of panic do what all other similar banks must do; that in time of panic it must advance freely and vigorously to the public out of the reserve.

And with the Bank of England, as with other Banks in the same case, these advances, if they are to be made at all, should be made so as if possible to obtain the object for which they are made. The end is to stay the panic; and the advances should, if possible, stay the panic. And for this purpose there are two rules: First. That these loans should only be made at a very high rate of interest This will operate as a heavy fine on unreasonable timidity, and will prevent the greatest number of applications by persons who do not require it. The rate should be raised early in the panic, so that the fine may be paid early; that no one may borrow out of idle precaution without paying well for it; that the Banking reserve may be protected as far as possible.

Secondly. That at this rate these advances should be made on all good banking securities, and as largely as the public ask for them. The reason is plain. The object is to stay alarm, and nothing therefore should be done to cause alarm. But the way to cause alarm is to refuse some one who has good security to offer. The news of this will spread in an instant through all the money market at a moment of terror; no one can say exactly who carries it, but in half an hour it will be carried on all sides, and will intensify the terror everywhere. No advances indeed need be made by which the Bank will ultimately lose. The amount of bad business in commercial countries is an infinitesimally small fraction of the whole business. That in a panic the bank, or banks, holding the ultimate reserve should refuse bad bills or bad securities will not make the panic really worse; the 'unsound' people are a feeble minority, and they are afraid even to look frightened for fear their unsoundness may be detected. The great majority, the majority to be protected, are the 'sound' people, the people who have good security to offer. If it is known that the Bank of England is freely advancing on what in ordinary times is reckoned a good securityon what is then commonly pledged and easily convertible--the alarm of the solvent merchants and bankers will be stayed. But if securities, really good and usually convertible, are refused by the Bank, the alarm will not abate, the other loans made will fail in obtaining their end, and the panic will become worse and worse.

It may be said that the reserve in the Banking Department will not be enough for all such loans. If that be so, the Banking Department must fail. But lending is, nevertheless, its best expedient. This is the method of making its money go the farthest, and of enabling it to get through the panic if anything will so enable it. Making no loans as we have seen will ruin it; making large loans and stopping, as we have also seen, will ruin it. The only safe plan for the Bank is the brave plan, to lend in a panic on every kind of current security, or every sort on which money is ordinarily and usually lent. This policy may not save the Bank; but if it do not, nothing will save it.

If we examine the manner in which the Bank of England has fulfilled these duties, we shall find, as we found before, that the true principle has never been grasped; that the policy has been inconsistent; that, though the policy has much improved, there still remain important particulars in which it might be better than it is. The first panic of which it is necessary here to speak, is that of 1825: I hardly think we should derive much instruction from those of 1793 and 1797; the world has changed too much since; and during the long period of inconvertible currency from 1797 to 1819, the problems to be solved were altogether different from our present ones. In the panic of 1825, the Bank of England at first acted as unwisely as it was possible to act. By every means it tried to restrict its advances. The reserve being very small, it endeavoured to protect that reserve by lending as little as possible. The result was a period of frantic and almost inconceivable violence; scarcely any one knew whom to trust; credit was almost suspended; the country was, as Mr. Huskisson expressed it, within twenty-four hours of a state of barter. Applications for assistance were made to the Government, but though it was well known that the Government refused to act, there was not, as far as I know, until lately any authentic narrative of the real facts. In the 'Correspondence' of the Duke of Wellington, of all places in the world, there is a full account of them. The Duke was then on a mission at St. Petersburg, and Sir R. Peel wrote to him a letter of which the following is a part: 'We have been placed in a very unpleasant predicament on the other question--the issue of Exchequer Bills by Government. The feeling of the City, of many of our friends, of some of the Opposition, was decidedly in favour of the issue of Exchequer Bills to relieve the merchants and manufacturers.

'It was said in favour of the issue, that the same measure had been tried and succeeded in 1793 and 1811. Our friends whispered about that we were acting quite in a different manner from that in which Mr. Pitt did act, and would have acted had he been alive.

'We felt satisfied that, however plausible were the reasons urged in favour of the issue of Exchequer Bills, yet that the measure was a dangerous one, and ought to be resisted by the Government.

'There are thirty millions of Exchequer Bills outstanding. The purchases lately made by the Bank can hardly maintain them at par. If there were a new issue to such an amount as that contemplated viz., five millions--there would be a great danger that the whole mass of Exchequer Bills would be at a discount, and would be paid into the revenue. If the new Exchequer Bills were to be issued at a different rate of interest from the outstanding onessay bearing an interest of five per cent--the old ones would be immediately at a great discount unless the interest were raised. If the interest were raised, the charge on the revenue would be of course proportionate to the increase of rate of interest. We found that the Bank had the power to lend money on deposit of goods. As our issue of Exchequer Bills would have been useless unless the Bank cashed them, as therefore the intervention of the Bank was in any event absolutely necessary, and as its intervention would be chiefly useful by the effect which it would have in increasing the circulating medium, we advised the Bank to take the whole affair into their own hands at once, to issue their notes on the security of goods, instead of issuing them on Exchequer Bills, such bills being themselves issued on that security.

'They reluctantly consented, and rescued us from a very embarrassing predicament.'

The success of the Bank of England on this occasion was owing to its complete adoption of right principles. The Bank adopted these principles very late; but when it adopted them it adopted them completely. According to the official statement which I quoted before, 'we,' that is, the Bank directors, 'lent money by every possible means, and in modes which we had never adopted before; we took in stock on security, we purchased Exchequer Bills, we made advances on Exchequer Bills, we not only discounted outright, but we made advances on deposits of bills of Exchange to an immense amountin short, by every possible means consistent with the safety of the Bank.' And for the complete and courageous adoption of this policy at the last moment the directors of the Bank of England at that time deserve great praise, for the subject was then less understood even than it is now; but the directors of the Bank deserve also severe censure, for previously choosing a contrary policy; for being reluctant to adopt the new one; and for at last adopting it only at the request of, and upon a joint responsibility with, the Executive Government.

After 1825, there was not again a real panic in the money market till 1847. Both of the crises of 1837 and 1839 were severe, but neither terminated in a panic: both were arrested before the alarm reached its final intensity; in neither, therefore, could the policy of the Bank at the last stage of fear be tested.

In the three panics since 1844--in 1847, 1857, and 1866--the policy of the Bank has been more or less affected by the Act of 1844, and I cannot therefore discuss it fully within the limits which I have pre scribed for myself. I can only state two things: First, that the directors of the Bank above all things maintain, that they have not been in the earlier stage of pamc prevented by the Act of 1844 from making any advances which they would otherwise have then made. Secondly, that in the last stage of panic, the Act of 1844 has been already suspended, rightly or wrongly, on these occasions; that no similar occasion has ever yet occurred in which it has not been suspended; and that, rightly or wrongly, the world confidently expects and relies that in all similar cases it will be suspended again. Whatever theory may prescribe, the logic of facts seems peremptory so far. And these principles taken together amount to saying that, by the doctrine of the directors, the Bank of England ought, as far as they can, to manage a panic with the Act of 1844, pretty much as they would manage one without it--in the early stage of the panic because then they are not fettered, and in the latter because then the fetter has been removed.

We can therefore estimate the policy of the Bank of England in the three panics which have happened since the Act of 1844, without inquiring into the effect of the Act itself. It is certain that in all of these panics the Bank has made very large advances indeed. It is certain, too, that in all of them the Bank has been quicker than it was in 1825; that in all of them it has less hesitated to use its banking reserve in making the advances which it is one principal object of maintaining that reserve to make, and to make at once. But there is still a considerable evil. No one knows on what kind of securities the Bank of England will at such periods make the advances which it is necessary to make.

As we have seen, principle requires that such advances, if made at all for the purpose of curing panic, should be made in the manner most likely to cure that panic. And for this purpose, they should be made on everything which in common times is good 'banking security.' The evil is, that owing to terror, what is commonly good security has ceased to be so; and the true policy is so to use the Banking reserve, that if possible the temporary evil may be stayed, and the common course of business be restored. And this can only be effected by advancing on all good Banking securities.

Unfortunately, the Bank of England do not take this course. The Discount office is open for the discount of good bills, and makes immense advances accordingly. The Bank also advances on consols and India securities, though there was, in the crisis of 1866, believed to be for a moment a hesitation in so doing. But these are only a small part of the securities on which money in ordinary times can be readily obtained, and by which its repayment is fully secured. Railway debenture stock is as good a security as a commercial bill, and many people, of whom I own I am one, think it safer than India stock; on the whole, a great railway is, we think, less liable to unforeseen accidents than the strange Empire of India. But I doubt if the Bank of England in a panic would advance on railway debenture stock, at any rate no one has any authorised reason for saying that it would. And there are many other such securities.

97

The amount of the advance is the main consideration for the Bank of England, and not the nature of the security on which the advance is made, always assuming the security to be good. An idea prevails (as I believe) at the Bank of England that they ought not to advance during a panic on any kind of security on which they do not commonly advance. But if bankers for the most part do advance on such security in common times, and if that security is indisputably good, the ordinary practice of the Bank of England is immaterial. In ordinary times the Bank is only one of many lenders, whereas in a panic it is the sole lender, and we want, as far as we can, to bring back the unusual state of a time of panic to the common state of ordinary times.

In common opinion there is always great uncertainty as to the conduct of the Bank: the Bank has never laid down any clear and sound policy on the subject. As we have seen, some of its directors (like Mr. Hankey) advocate an erroneous policy. The public is never sure what policy will be adopted at the most important moment: it is not sure what amount of advance will be made, or on what security it will be made. The best palliative to a panic is a confidence in the adequate amount of the Bank reserve, and in the efficient use of that reserve. And until we have on this point a clear understanding with the Bank of England, both our liability to crises and our terror at crises will always be greater than they would otherwise be.

CHAPTER VIII.

The Government of the Bank of England.

The Bank of England is governed by a board of directors, a Governor, and a Deputy-Governor; and the mode in which these are chosen, and the time for which they hold office, affect the whole of its business. The board of directors is in fact self-electing. In theory a certain portion go out annually, remain out for a year, and are subject to re-election by the proprietors. But in fact they are nearly always, and always if the other directors wish it, re-elected after a year. Such has been the unbroken practice of many years, and it would be hardly possible now to break it. When a vacancy occurs by death or resignation, the whole board chooses the new member, and they do it, as I am told, with great care. For a peculiar reason, it is important that the directors should be young when they begin; and accordingly the board run over the names of the most attentive and promising young men in the old-established firms of London, and select the one who, they think, will be most suitable for a bank director. There is a considerable ambition to fill the office. The status which is given by it, both to the individual who fills it and to the firm of merchants to which he belongs, is considerable. There is surprisingly little favour shown in the selection; there is a great wish on the part of the Bank directors for the time being to provide, to the best of their ability, for the future good government of the Bank. Very few selections in the world are made with nearly equal purity. There is a sincere desire to do the best for the Bank, and to appoint a well-conducted young man who has begun to attend to business, and who seems likely to be fairly sensible and fairly efficient twenty years later.

The age is a primary matter. The offices of Governor and Deputy-Governor are given in rotation. The Deputy-Governor always succeeds the Governor, and usually the oldest director who has not been m office becomes Deputy-Governor. Sometimes, from personal reasons, such as ill-health or special temporary occupation, the time at which a director becomes Deputy-Governor may be a little deferred, and, in some few cases, merchants in the greatest business have been permitted to decline entirely. But for all general purposes, the rule may be taken as absolute. Save in rare cases, a director must serve his time as Governor and Deputy-Governor nearly when his turn comes, and he will not be asked to serve much before his turn. It is usually about twenty years from the time of a man's first election that he arrives, as it is called, at the chair. And as the offices of Governor and Deputy-Governor are very important, a man who fills them should be still in the vigour of life. Accordingly, Bank directors, when first chosen by the board, are always young men.

At first this has rather a singular effect; a stranger hardly knows what to make of it. Many years since, I remember seeing a very fresh and nice-looking young gentleman, and being struck with astonishment at being told that he was a director of the Bank of England. I had always imagined such directors to be men of tried sagacity and long experience, and I was amazed that a cheerful young man should be one of them. I believe I thought it was a little dangerous. I thought such young men could not manage the Bank well. I feared they had the power to do mischief.

Further inquiry, however, soon convinced me that they had not the power. Naturally, young men have not much influence at a board where there, are many older members. And in the Bank of England there is a special provision for depriving them of it if they get it. Some of the directors, as I have said, retire annually, but by courtesy it is always the young ones. Those who have passed the chair--that is, who have served the office of Governor--always remain. The young part of the board is the fluctuating part, and the old part is the permanent part; and therefore it is not surprising that the young part has little influence. The Bank directors may be blamed for many things, but they cannot be blamed for the changeableness and excitability of a neocracy.

Indeed, still better to prevent it, the elder members of the board that is, those who have passed the chairform a standing committee of indefinite powers, which is called the Committee of Treasury. I say 'indefinite powers,' for I am not aware that any precise description has ever been given of them, and I doubt if they can be precisely described. They are sometimes said to exercise a particular control over the relations and negotiations between the Bank and the Government. But I confess that I believe that this varies very much with the character of the Governor for the time being. A strong Governor does much mainly upon his own responsibility, and a weak Governor does little. Still the influence of the Committee of Treasury is always considerable, though not always the same. They form a a cabinet of mature, declining, and old men, just close to the executive; and for good or evil such a cabinet must have much power.

By old usage, the directors of the Bank of England cannot be themselves by trade bankers. This is a relic of old times. Every bank was supposed to be necessarily, more or less, in opposition to every other bankbanks in the same place to be especially in opposition. In consequence, in London, no banker has a chance of being a Bank director, or would ever think of attempting to be one. I am here speaking of bankers in the English sense, and in the sense that would surprise a foreigner. One of the Rothschilds is on the Bank direction, and a foreigner would be apt to think that they were bankers if any one was. But this only illustrates the essential difference between our English notions of banking and the continental. Ours have attained a much fuller development than theirs. Messrs. Rothschild are immense capitalists, having, doubtless, much borrowed money in their hands. But they do not take 100 L. payable on demand, and pay it back in cheques of 5 L. each, and that is our English banking. The borrowed money which they have is in large sums, borrowed for terms more or less long. English bankers deal with an aggregate of small sums, all of which are repayable on short notice, or on demand. And the way the two employ their money is different also. A foreigner thinks 'an Exchange business'that is, the buying and selling bills on foreign countriesa main part of banking. As I have explained, remittance is one of the subsidiary conveniences which early banks subserve before deposit banking begins. But the mass of English country bankers only give bills on places in England or on London, and in London the principal remittance business has escaped out of the hands of the bankers. Most of them would not know how to carry through a great 'Exchange operation,' or to 'bring home the returns.' They would as soon think of turning silk merchants. The Exchange trade is carried on by a small and special body of foreign bill-brokers, of whom Messrs. Rothschild are the greatest. One of that firm may, therefore, well be on the Bank direction, notwithstanding the rule forbidding bankers to be there, for he and his family are not English bankers, either by the terms on which they borrow money, or the mode in which they employ it. But as to bankers in the English sense of the word, the rule is rigid and absolute. Not only no private banker is a director of the Bank of England, but no director of any joint stock bank would be allowed to become such. The two situations would be taken to be incompatible.

The mass of the Bank directors are merchants of experience, employing a considerable capital in trades in which they have been brought up, and with which they are well acquainted. Many of them have information as to the present course of trade, and as to the character and wealth of merchants, which is most valuable, or rather is all but invaluable, to the Bank. Many of them, too, are quiet, serious men, who, by habit and nature, watch with some kind of care every kind of business in which they are engaged, and give an anxious opinion on it. Most of them have a good deal of leisure, for the life of a man of business who employs only his own capital, and employs it nearly always in the same way, is by no means fully employed. Hardly any capital is enough to employ the principal partner's time, and if such a man is very busy, it is a sign of something wrong. Either he is working at detail, which subordinates would do better, and which he had better leave alone, or he is engaged in too many speculations, is incurring more liabilities than his capital will bear, and so may be ruined. In consequence, every commercial city abounds in men who have great business ability and experience, who are not fully occupied, who wish to be occupied, and who are very glad to become directors of public companies in order to be occupied. The direction of the Bank of England has, for many generations, been composed of such men.

Such a government for a joint stock company is very good if its essential nature be attended to, and very bad if that nature be not attended to. That government is composed of men with a high average of general good sense, with an excellent knowledge of business in general, but without any special knowledge of the particular business in which they are engaged. Ordinarily, in joint stock banks and companies this deficiency is cured by the selection of a manager of the company, who has been specially trained to that particular trade, and who engages to devote all his experience and all his ability to the affairs of the company. The directors, and often a select committee of them more especially, consult with the manager, and after hearing what he has to say, decide on the affairs of the company. There is in all ordinary joint stock companies a fixed executive specially skilled, and a somewhat varying council not specially skilled. The fixed manager ensures continuity and experience in the management, and a good board of directors ensures general wisdom.

But in the Bank of England there is no fixed executive. The Governor and Deputy-Governor, who form that executive, change every two years. I believe, indeed, that such was not the original intention of the founders. In the old days of few and great privileged companies, the chairman, though periodically elected, was practically permanent so long as his policy was popular. He was the head of the ministry, and ordinarily did not change unless the opposition came in. But this idea has no present relation to the constitution of the Bank of England. At present, the Governor and Deputy-Governor almost always change at the end of two years; the case of any longer occupation of the chair is so very rare, that it need not be taken account of. And the Governor and Deputy-Governor of the Bank cannot well be shadows. They are expected to be constantly present; to see all applicants for advances out of the ordinary routine; to carry on the almost continuous correspondence between the Bank and its largest customer--the Government; to bring all necessary matters before the board of directors or the Committee of Treasury, in a word, to do very much of what falls to the lot of the manager in most companies. Under this shifting chief executive, there are indeed very valuable heads of departments. The head of the Discount Department is especially required to be a man of ability and experience. But these officers are essentially subordinate; no one of them is like the general manager of an ordinary bankthe head of all action. The perpetually present executive--the Governor and Deputy-Governor--make it impossible that any subordinate should have that position. A really able and active-minded Governor, being required to sit all day in the bank, in fact does, and can hardly help doing, its principal business.

In theory, nothing can be worse than this government for a bank a shifting executive; a board of directors chosen too young for it to be known whether they are able; a committee of management, in which seniority is the necessary qualification, and old age the common result; and no trained bankers anywhere.

Even if the Bank of England were an ordinary bank, such a constitution would be insufficient; but its inadequacy is greater, and the consequences of that inadequacy far worse, because of its greater functions. The Bank of England has to keep the sole banking reserve of the country; has to keep it through all changes of the money market, and all turns of the Exchanges; has to decide on the instant in a panic what sort of advances should be made, to what amounts, and for what dates; and yet it has a constitution plainly defective. So far the government of the Bank of England being better than that of any other bankas it ought to be, considering that its functions are much harder and graver--any one would be laughed at who proposed it as a model for the government of a new bank; and that government, if it were so proposed, would on all hands be called old-fashioned, and curious.

As was natural, the effects--good and evil--of its constitution are to be seen in every part of the Bank's history. On one vital point the Bank's management has been excellent. It has done perhaps less 'bad business,' certainly less very bad business, than any bank of the same size and the same age. In all its history I do not know that its name has ever been connected with a single large and discreditable bad debt. There has never been a suspicion that it was 'worked' for the benefit of any one man, or any combination of men. The great respectability of the directors, and the steady attention many of them have always given the business of the Bank, have kept it entirely free from anything dishonorable and discreditable. Steady merchants collected in council are an admirable judge of bills and securities. They always know the questionable standing of dangerous persons; they are quick to note the smallest signs of corrupt transactions; and no sophistry will persuade the best of them out of their good instincts. You could not have made the directors of the Bank of England do the sort of business which 'Overends' at last did, except by a moral miracle--except by changing their nature. And the fatal career of the Bank of the United States would, under their management, have been equally impossible. Of the ultimate solvency of the Bank of England, or of the eventual safety of its vast capital, even at the worst periods of its history, there has not been the least doubt.

But nevertheless, as we have seen, the policy of the Bank has frequently been deplorable, and at such times the defects of its government have aggravated if not caused its calamities.

In truth the executive of the Bank of England is now much such as the executive of a public department of the Foreign Office or the Home Office would be in which there was no responsible permanent head. In these departments of Government, the actual chief changes nearly, though not quite, as often as the Governor of the Bank of England. The Parliamentary Under-Secretary--the Deputy-Governor, so to speak, of that office--changes nearly as often. And if the administration solely, or in its details, depended on these two, it would stop. New men could not carry it on with vigour and efficiency; indeed they could not carry it on at all. But, in fact, they are assisted by a permanent Under-Secretary, who manages all the routine business, who is the depository of the secrets of the office, who embodies its traditions, who is the hyphen between changing administrations. In consequence of this assistance, the continuous business of the department is, for the most part, managed sufficiently well, notwithstanding frequent changes in the heads of administration. And it is only by such assistance that such business could be so managed. The present administration of the Bank is an attempt to manage a great, a growing, and a permanently continuous business without an adequate permanent element, and a competent connecting link.

In answer, it may be said that the duties which press on the Governor and Deputy-Governor of the Bank are not so great or so urgent as those which press upon the heads of official departments. And perhaps, in point of mere labour, the Governor of the Bank has the advantage. Banking never ought to be an exceedingly laborious trade. There must be a great want of system and a great deficiency in skilled assistance if extreme labour is thrown upon the chief. But in importance, the functions of the head of the Bank rank as high as those of any department. The cash reserve of the country is as precious a deposit as any set of men can have the care of. And the difficulty of dealing with a panic (as the administration of the Bank is forced to deal with it) is perhaps a more formidable instant difficulty than presses upon any single minister. At any rate, it comes more suddenly, and must be dealt with more immediately, than most comparable difficulties; and the judgment, the nerve, and the vigour needful to deal with it are plainly rare and great.

The natural remedy would be to appoint a permanent Governor of the Bank. Nor, as I have said, can there be much doubt that such was the intention of its founders. All the old companies which have their beginning in the seventeenth century had the same constitution, and those of them which have lingered down to our time retain it. The Hudson's Bay Company, the South Sea Company, the East India Company, were all founded with a sort of sovereign executive, intended to be permanent, and intended to be efficient. This is, indeed, the most natural mode of forming a company in the minds of those to whom companies are new. Such persons will have always seen business transacted a good deal despotically; they will have learnt the value of prompt decision and of consistent policy; they will have often seen that business is best managed when those who are conducting it could scarcely justify the course they are pursuing by distinct argument which others could understand. All 'city' people make their money by investments, for which there are often good argumentative reasons; but they would hardly ever be able, if required before a Parliamentary committee, to state those reasons. They have become used to act on them without distinctly analysing them, and, in a monarchical way, with continued success only as a test of their goodness. Naturally such persons, when proceeding to form a company, make it upon the model of that which they have been used to see successful. They provide for the executive first and above all things. How much this was in the minds of the founders of the Bank of England may be judged of by the name which they gave it. Its corporate name is the 'Governor and Company of the Bank of England.' So important did the founders think the executive that they mentioned it distinctly, and mentioned it first.

And not only is this constitution of a company the most natural in the early days when companies were new, it is also that which experience has shown to be the most efficient now that companies have long been tried. Great railway companies are managed upon no other. Scarcely any instance of great success in a railway can be mentioned in which the chairman has not been an active and judicious man of business, constantly attending to the affairs of the company. A thousand instances of railway disaster can be easily found in which the chairman was only a nominal heada nobleman, or something of that sort-chosen for show. 'Railway chairmanship' has become a profession, so much is efficiency valued in it, and so indispensable has ability been found to be. The plan of appointing a permanent 'chairman' at the Bank of England is strongly supported by much modern experience.

Nevertheless, I hesitate as to its expediency; at any rate, there are other plans which, for several reasons, should, I think, first be tried in preference.

First. This plan would be exceedingly unpopular. A permanent Governor of the Bank of England would be one of the greatest men in England. He would be a little 'monarch' in the City; he would be far greater than the 'Lord Mayor.' He would be the personal embodiment of the Bank of England; he would be constantly clothed with an almost indefinite prestige. Everybody in business would bow down before him and try to stand well with him, for he might in a panic be able to save almost anyone he liked, and to ruin almost anyone he liked. A day might come when his favour might mean prosperity, and his distrust might mean ruin. A position with so much real power and so much apparent dignity would be intensely coveted. Practical men would be apt to say that it was better than the Prime Ministership, for it would last much longer, and would have a greater jurisdiction over that which practical men would most value, over money. At all events, such a Governor, if he understood his business, might make the fortunes of fifty men where the Prime Minister can make that of one. Scarcely anything could be more unpopular in the City than the appointment of a little king to reign over them.

Secondly. I do not believe that we should always get the best man for the post; often I fear that we should not even get a tolerable man. There are many cases in which the offer of too high a pay would prevent our obtaining the man we wish for, and this is one of them. A very high pay of prestige is almost always very dangerous. It causes the post to be desired by vain men, by lazy men, by men of rank; and when that post is one of real and technical business, and when, therefore, it requires much previous training, much continuous labour, and much patient and quick judgment, all such men are dangerous. But they are sure to covet all posts of splendid dignity, and can only be kept out of them with the greatest difficulty. Probably, in every Cabinet there are still some members (in the days of the old close boroughs there were many) whose posts have come to them not from personal ability or inherent merit, but from their rank, their wealth, or even their imposing exterior. The highest political offices are, indeed, kept clear of such people, for in them serious and important duties must constantly be performed in the face of the world. A Prime Minister, or a Chancellor of the Exchequer, or a Secretary of State must explain his policy and defend his actions in Parliament, and the discriminating tact of a critical assemblyabounding in experience, and guided by traditionwill soon discover what he is. But the Governor of the Bank would only perform quiet functions, which look like routine, though they are not, m which there is no immediate risk of success or failure; which years hence may indeed issue in a crop of bad debts, but which any grave persons may make at the time to look fair and plausible. A large Bank is exactly the place where a vain and shallow person in authority, if he be a man of gravity and method, as such men often are, may do infinite evil in no long time, and before he is detected. If he is lucky enough to begin at a time of expansion in trade, he is nearly sure not to be found out till the time of contraction has arrived, and then very large figures will be required to reckon the evil he has done.

And thirdly, I fear that the possession of such patronage would ruin any set of persons in whose gift it was. The election of the Chairman must be placed either in the court of proprietors or that of the directors. If the proprietors choose, there will be something like the evils of an American presidential election. Bank stock will be bought in order to confer the qualification of voting at the election of the 'chief of the City.' The Chairman, when elected, may well find that his most active supporters are large borrowers of the Bank, and he may well be puzzled to decide between his duty to the Bank and his gratitude to those who chose him. Probably, if he be a cautious man of average ability, he will combine both evils; he will not lend so much money as he is asked for, and so will offend his own supporters; but will lend some which will be lost, and so the profits of the Bank will be reduced. A large body of Bank proprietors would make but a bad elective body for an office of great prestige; they would not commonly choose a good person, and the person they did choose would be bound by promises that would make him less good.

The court of directors would choose better; a small body of men of business would not easily be persuaded to choose an extremely unfit man. But they would not often choose an extremely good man. The really best man would probably not be so rich as the majority of the directors, nor of so much standing, and not unnaturally they would much dislike to elevate to the headship of the City, one who was much less in the estimation of the City than themselves. And they would be canvassed in every way and on every side to appoint a man of mercantile dignity or mercantile influence. Many people of the greatest prestige and rank in the City would covet so great a dignity; if not for themselves, at least for some friend, or some relative, and so the directors would be set upon from every side.

An election so liable to be disturbed by powerful vitiating causes would rarely end in a good choice. The best candidate would almost never be chosen; often, I fear, one would be chosen altogether unfit for a post so important. And the excitement of so keen an election would altogether disturb the quiet of the Bank. The good and efficient working of a board of Bank directors depends on its internal harmony, and that harmony would be broken for ever by the excitement, the sayings, and the acts of a great election. The board of directors would almost certainly be demoralised by having to choose a sovereign, and there is no certainty, nor any great likelihood, indeed, that they would choose a good one. In France the difficulty of finding a good body to choose the Governor of the Bank has been met characteristically. The Bank of France keeps the money of the State, and the State appoints its governor. The French have generally a logical reason to give for all they do, though perhaps the results of their actions are not always so good as the reasons for them. The Governor of the Bank of France has not always, I am told, been a very competent person; the Sub-Governor, whom the State also appoints, is, as we might expect, usually better. But for our English purposes it would be useless to inquire minutely into this. No English statesman would consent to be responsible for the choice of the Governor of the Bank of England. After every panic, the Opposition would say in Parliament that the calamity had been 'grievously aggravated,' if not wholly caused, by the 'gross misconduct' of the Governor appointed by the ministry. Or, possibly, offices may have changed occupants and the ministry in power at the panic would be the opponents of the ministry which at a former time appointed the Governor. In that case they would be apt to feel, and to intimate, a 'grave regret' at the course which the nominee of their adversaries had 'thought it desirable to pursue.' They would not much mind hurting his feelings, and if he resigned they would have themselves a valuable piece of patronage to confer on one of their own friends. No result could be worse than that the conduct of the Bank and the management should be made a matter of party politics, and men of all parties would agree in this, even if they agreed in almost nothing else.

I am therefore afraid that we must abandon the plan of improving the government of the Bank of England by the appointment of a permanent Governor, because we should not be sure of choosing a good governor, and should indeed run a great risk, for the most part, of choosing a bad one.

I think, however, that much of the advantage, with little of the risk, might be secured by a humbler scheme. In English political offices, as was observed before, the evil of a changing head is made possible by the permanence of a dignified subordinate. Though the Parliamentary Secretary of State and the Parliamentary Under-Secretary go in and out with each administration, another Under-Secretary remains through all such changes, and is on that account called 'permanent.' Now this system seems to me in its principle perfectly applicable to the administration of the Bank of England. For the reasons which have just been given, a permanent ruler of the Bank of England cannot be appointed; for other reasons, which were just before given, some most influential permanent functionary is essential in the proper conduct of the business of the Bank; and, mutatis mutandis, these are the very difficulties, and the very advantages which have led us to frame our principal offices of state in the present fashion.

Such a Deputy-Governor would not be at all a 'king' in the City. There would be no mischievous prestige about the office; there would be no attraction in it for a vain man; and there would be nothing to make it an object of a violent canvass or of unscrupulous electioneering. The office would be essentially subordinate in its character, just like the permanent secretary in a political office. The pay should be high, for good ability is wanted--but no pay would attract the most dangerous class of people. The very influential, but not very wise, City dignitary who would be so very dangerous is usually very opulent; he would hardly have such influence he were not opulent: what he wants is not money, but 'position.' A Governorship of the Bank of England he would take almost without salary; perhaps he would even pay to get it: but a minor office of essential subordination would not attract him at all. We may augment the pay enough to get a good man, without fearing that by such pay we may temptas by social privilege we should temptexactly the sort of man we do not want.

Undoubtedly such a permanent official should be a trained banker. There is a cardinal difference between banking and other kinds of commerce; you can afford to run much less risk in banking than in commerce, and you must take much greater precautions. In common business, the trader can add to the cost price of the goods he sells a large mercantile profit, say 10 to 15 per cent; but the banker has to be content with the interest of money, which in England is not so much as per cent upon the average. The business of a banker therefore cannot bear so many bad debts as that of a merchant, and he must be much more cautious to whom he gives credit. Real money is a commodity much more coveted than common goods: for one deceit which is attempted on a manufacturer or a merchant, twenty or more are attempted on a banker. And besides, a banker, dealing with the money of others, and money payable on demand, must be always, as it were, looking behind him and seeing that he has reserve enough in store if payment should be asked for, which a merchant dealing mostly with his own capital need not think of. Adventure is the life of commerce, but caution, I had almost said timidity, is the life of banking; and I cannot imagine that the long series of great errors made by the Bank of England in the management of its reserve till after 1857, would have been possible if the merchants in the Bank court had not erroneously taken the same view of the Bank's business that they must properly take of their own mercantile business. The Bank directors have almost always been too cheerful as to the Bank's business, and too little disposed to take alarm. What we want to introduce into the Bank court is a wise apprehensiveness, and this every trained banker is taught by the habits of his trade, and the atmosphere of his life.

The permanent Governor ought to give his whole time to the business of the Bank. He ought to be forbidden to engage in any other concern. All the present directors, including the Governor and Deputy-Governor, are engaged in their own business, and it is very possible, indeed it must perpetually have happened, that their own business as merchants most occupied the minds of most of them just when it was most important that the business of the Bank should occupy them. It is at a panic and just before a panic that the business of the Bank is most exacting and most engrossing. But just at that time the business of most merchants must be unusually occupying and may be exceedingly critical. By the present constitution of the Bank, the attention of its sole rulers is most apt to be diverted from the Bank's affairs just when those affairs require that attention the most. And the only remedy is the appointment of a permanent and influential man, who will have no business save that of the Bank, and who therefore presumably will attend most to it at the critical instant when attention is most required. His mind, at any rate, will in a panic be free from pecuniary anxiety, whereas many, if not all, of the present directors must be incessantly thinking of their own affairs and unable to banish them from their minds.

The permanent Deputy-Governor must be a director and a man of fair position. He must not have to say 'Sir' to the Governor. There is no fair argument between an inferior who has to exhibit respect and a superior who has to receive respect. The superior can always, and does mostly, refute the bad arguments of his inferior; but the inferior rarely ventures to try to refute the bad arguments of his superior. And he still more rarely states his case effectually; he pauses, hesitates, does not use the best word or the most apt illustration, perhaps he uses a faulty illustration or a wrong word, and so fails because the superior immediately exposes him. Important business can only be sufficiently discussed by persons who can say very much what they like very much as they like to one another. The thought of the speaker should come out as it was in his mind, and not be hidden in respectful expressions or enfeebled by affected doubt. What is wanted at the Bank is not a new clerk to the directors, they have excellent clerks of great experience nowbut a permanent equal to the directors, who shall be able to discuss on equal terms with them the business of the Bank, and have this advantage over them in discussion, that he has no other business than that of the Bank to think of.

The formal duties of such a permanent officer could only be defined by some one conversant with the business of the Bank, and could scarcely be intelligibly discussed before the public. Nor are the precise duties of the least importance. Such an officer, if sound, able, and industrious, would soon rule the affairs of the Bank. He would be acquainted better than anyone else, both with the traditions of the past and with the facts of the present; he would have a great experience; he would have seen many anxious times; he would always be on the watch for their recurrence. And he would have a peculiar power of guidance at such moments from the nature of the men with whom he has most to deal. Most Governors of the Bank of England are cautious merchants, not profoundly skilled in banking, but most anxious that their period of office should be prosperous and that they should themselves escape censure. If a 'safe' course is pressed upon them they are likely to take that course. Now it would almost always be 'safe' to follow the advice of the great standing 'authority'; it would always be most 'unsafe' not to follow it. If the changing Governor act on the advice of the permanent Deputy-Governor, most of the blame in case of mischance would fall on the latter; it would be said that a shifting officer like the Governor might very likely not know what should be done, but that the permanent official was put there to know it and paid to know it. But if, on the other hand, the changing Governor should disregard the advice of his permanent colleague, and the consequence should be bad, he would be blamed exceedingly. It would be said that, 'being without experience, he had taken upon him to overrule men who had much experience; that when the constitution of the Bank had provided them with skilled counsel, he had taken on himself to act of his own head, and to disregard that counsel;' and so on ad infinitum. And there could be no sort of conversation more injurious to a man in the City; the world there would say, rightly or wrongly, 'We must never be too severe on errors of judgment; we are all making them every day; if responsible persons do their best we can expect no more. But this case is different: the Governor acted on a wrong system; he took upon himself an unnecessary responsibility:' and so a Governor who incurred disaster by disregarding his skilled counsellor would be thought a fool in the City for ever. In consequence, the one skilled counsellor would in fact rule the Bank. I believe that the appointment of the new permanent and skilled authority at the Bank is the greatest reform which can be made there, and that which is most wanted. I believe that such a person would give to the decision of the Bank that foresight, that quickness, and that consistency m which those decisions are undeniably now deficient. As far as I can judge, this change in the constitution of the Bank is by far the most necessary, and is perhaps more important even than all other changes. But, nevertheless, we should reform the other points which we have seen to be defective.

First, the London bankers should not be altogether excluded from the court of directors. The old idea, as I have explained, was that the London bankers were the competitors of the Bank of England, and would hurt it if they could. But now the London bankers have another relation to the Bank which did not then exist, and was not then imagined. Among private people they are the principal depositors in the Bank; they are therefore particularly interested in its stability; they are especially interested in the maintenance of a good banking reserve, for their own credit and the safety of their large deposits depend on it. And they can bring to the court of directors an experience of banking itself, got outside the Bank of England, which none of the present directors possess, for they have learned all they know of banking at the Bank itself. There was also an old notion that the secrets of the Bank would be divulged if they were imparted to bankers. But probably bankers are better trained to silence and secrecy than most people. And there is only a thin partition now between the bankers and the secrets of the Bank. Only lately a firm failed of which one partner was a director of the London and Westminster Bank, and another a director of the Bank of England. Who can define or class the confidential communications of such persons under such circumstances?

As I observed before, the line drawn at present against bankers is very technical and exclusively English. According to continental ideas, Messrs. Rothschild are bankers, if any one is a banker. But the house of Rothschild is represented on the Bank direction. And it is most desirable that it should be represented, for members of that firm can give if they choose confidential information of great value to the Bank. But, nevertheless, the objection which is urged against English bankers is at least equally applicable to these foreign bankers. They have, or may have, at certain periods an interest opposite to the policy of the Bank. As the greatest Exchange dealers, they may wish to export gold just when the Bank of England is raising its rate of interest to prevent anyone from exporting gold. The vote of a great Exchange dealer might be objected to for plausible reasons of contrary interest, if any such reasons were worth regarding. But in fact the particular interest of single directors is not to be regarded; almost all directors who bring special information labour under a suspicion of interest; they can only have acquired that information in present business, and such business may very possibly be affected for good or evil by the policy of the Bank. But you must not on this account seal up the Bank hermetically against living information; you must make a fair body of directors upon the whole, and trust that the bias of some individual interests will disappear and be lost in the whole. And if this is to be the guiding principle, it is not consistent to exclude English bankers from the court.

Objection is often also taken to the constitution of the Committee of Treasury. That body is composed of the Governor and Deputy-Governor and all the directors who have held those offices; but as those offices in the main pass in rotation, this mode of election very much comes to an election by seniority, and there are obvious objections to giving, not only a preponderance to age, but a monopoly to age. In some cases, indeed, this monopoly I believe has already been infringed. When directors have on account of the magnitude of their transactions, and the consequent engrossing nature of their business, declined to fill the chair, in some cases they have been asked to be members of the Committee of Treasury notwithstanding. And it would certainly upon principle seem wiser to choose a committee which for some purposes approximates to a committee of management by competence rather than by seniority.

An objection is also taken to the large number of Bank directors. There are twenty-four directors, a Governor and a Deputy-Governor, making a total court of twenty-six persons, which is obviously too large for the real discussion of any difficult business. And the case is worse because the court only meets once a week, and only sits a very short time. It has been said, with exaggeration, but not without a basis of truth, that if the Bank directors were to sit for four hours, there would be 'a panic solely from that.' 'The court,' says Mr. Tooke, 'meets at half-past eleven or twelve; and, if the sitting be prolonged beyond half-past one, the Stock Exchange and the money market become excited, under the idea that a change of importance is under discussion; and persons congregate about the doors of the Bank parlour to obtain the earliest intimation of the decision.' And he proceeds to conjecture that the knowledge of the impatience without must cause haste, if not impatience, within. That the decisions of such a court should be of incalculable importance is plainly very strange.

There should be no delicacy as to altering the constitution of the Bank of England. The existing constitution was framed in times that have passed away, and was intended to be used for purposes very different from the present. The founders may have considered that it would lend money to the Government, that it would keep the money of the Government, that it would issue notes payable to bearer, but that it would keep the 'Banking reserve' of a great nation no one in the seventeenth century imagined. And when the use to which we are putting an old thing is a new use, in common sense we should think whether the old thing is quite fit for the use to which we are setting it. 'Putting new wine into old bottles' is safe only when you watch the condition of the bottle, and adapt its structure most carefully.

CHAPTER IX.

The Joint Stock Banks.

The Joint Stock Banks of this country are a most remarkable success. Generally speaking the career of Joint Stock Companies in this country has been chequered. Adam Smith, many years since, threw out many pregnant hints on the difficulty of such undertakings--hints which even after so many years will well repay perusal. But joint stock banking has been an exception to this rule. Four years ago I threw together the facts on the subject and the reasons for them; and I venture to quote the article, because subsequent experience suggests, I think, little to be added to it.

'The main classes of joint stock companies which have answered are three:--1st. Those in which the capital is used not to work the business but to guarantee the business. Thus a banker's business--his proper business--does not begin while he is using his own money: it commences when he begins to use the capital of others. An insurance office in the long run needs no capital; the premiums which are received ought to exceed the claims which accrue. In both cases, the capital is wanted to assure the public and to induce it to trust the concern. 2ndly. Those companies have answered which have an exclusive privilege which they have used with judgment, or which possibly was so very profitable as to enable them to thrive with little judgment. 3rdly. Those which have undertaken a business both large and simple--employing more money than most individuals or private firms have at command, and yet such that, in Adam Smith's words, 'the operations are capable of being reduced to a routine or such an uniformity of method as admits of no variation."

'As a rule, the most profitable of these companies are banks. Indeed, all the favouring conditions just mentioned concur in many banks. An old-established bank has a "prestige," which amounts to a "privileged opportunity"; though no exclusive right is given to it by law, a peculiar power is given to it by opinion. The business of banking ought to be simple; if it is hard it is wrong. The only securities which a banker, using money that he may be asked at short notice to repay, ought to touch, are those which are easily saleable and easily intelligible. If there is a difficulty or a doubt, the security should be declined. No business can of course be quite reduced to fixed rules. There must be occasional cases which no pre-conceived theory can define. But banking comes as near to fixed rules certainly as any existing business, perhaps as any possible business. The business of an old-established bank has the full advantage of being a simple business, and in part the advantage of being a monopoly business. Competition with it is only open in the sense in which competition with "the London Tavern" is open; anyone that has to do with either will pay dear for it.

'But the main source of the profitableness of established banking is the smallness of the requisite capital. Being only wanted as a "moral influence," it need not be more than is necessary to secure that influence. Although, therefore, a banker deals only with the most sure securities, and with those which yield the least interest, he can nevertheless gain and divide a very large profit upon his own capital, because the money in his hands is so much larger than that capital.

'Experience, as shown by plain figures, confirms these conclusions. We print at the end of this article the respective profits of 110 banks in England, and Scotland, and Ireland, being all in those countries of which we have sufficient information--the Bank of England excepted. There are no doubt others, but they are not quoted even on local Stock Exchange lists, and in most cases publish no reports. The result of these banks, as regards the dividends they pay, is--

	No. of Companies	Capital L
Above 20 per cent	15	5,302,767
Between 15 and 20 per cent	20	5,439,439
10 and 15 per cent	36	14,056,950
5 and 10 per cent	36	14,182,379
Under 5 per cent	3	1,350,000
	110	40,331,535

that is to say, above 25 per cent of the capital employed in these banks pays over 15 per cent, and 62 1/2 per cent of the capital pays more than 10 per cent. So striking a result is not to be shown in any other joint stock trade.

'The period to which these accounts refer was certainly not a particularly profitable oneon the contrary, it has been specially unprofitable. The rate of interest has been very low, and the amount of good security in the market small. Many banks--to some extent most banks--probably had in their books painful reminiscences of 1866. The fever of excitement which passed over the nation was strongest in the classes to whom banks lent most, and consequently the losses of even the most careful banks (save of those in rural and sheltered situations) were probably greater than usual. But even tried by this very unfavourable test banking is a trade profitable far beyond the average of trades.

'There is no attempt in these banks on the whole and as a rule to divide too muchon the contrary, they have accumulated about 13,000,000 L., or nearly 1/3 rd of their capital, principally out of undivided profits. The directors of some of them have been anxious to put away as much as possible and to divide as little as possible.

'The reason is plain; out of the banks which pay more than 20 per cent, all but one were old-established banks, and all those paying between 15 and 20 per cent were old banks too. The "privileged opportunity" of which we spoke is singularly conspicuous in such figures; it enables banks to pay much, which without it would not have paid much. The amount of the profit is clearly proportional to the value of the "privileged opportunity." All the banks which pay above 20 per cent, save one, are banks more than 25 years old; all those which pay between 15 and 20 are so too. A new bank could not make these profits, or even by its competition much reduce these profits; in attempting to do so, it would simply ruin itself. Not possessing the accumulated credit of years, it would have to wind up before it attained that credit.

'The value of the opportunity too is proportioned to what has to be paid for it. Some old banks have to pay interest for all their money; some have much for which they pay nothing. Those who give much to their customers have of course less left for their shareholders. Thus Scotland, where there is always a daily interest, has no bank in the lists paying over 15 per cent. The profits of Scotch banks run thus:

	Capital L	Dividend
Bank of Scotland	1,500,000	12
British Linen Company	1,000,000	3
Caledonian	125,000	10
Clydesdale	900,000	10
Commercial Bank of Scotland	1,000,000	13
National Bank of Scotland	1,000,000	112
North of Scotland	280,000	10
Union Bank of Scotland	1,000,000	10
City of Glasgow	870,000	8
Royal Bank	2,000,000	8
	9,675,000	

Good profits enough, but not at all like the profits of the London and Westminster, or the other most lucrative banks of the South.

'The Bank of England, it is true, does not seem to pay so much as other English banks in this way of reckoning. It makes an immense profit, but then its capital is immense too. In fact, the Bank of England suffers under two difficulties. Being much older than the other joint stock banks, it belongs to a less profitable era. When it was founded, banks looked rather to the profit on their own capital, and to the gains of note issue than to the use of deposits. The first relations with the State were more like those of a finance company than of a bank, as we now think of banking. If the Bank had not made loans to the Government, which we should now think dubious, the Bank would not have existed, for the Government would never have permitted it. Not only is the capital of the Bank of England relatively greater, but the means of making profit in the Bank of England are relatively less also. By custom and understanding the Bank of England keep a much greater reserve in unprofitable cash than other banks; if they do not keep it, either our whole system must be changed or we should break up in utter bankruptcy. The earning faculty of the Bank of England is in proportion less than that of other banks, and also the sum on which it has to pay dividend is altogether greater than theirs.

'It is interesting to compare the facts of joint stock banking with the fears of it which were felt. In 1832, Lord Overstone observed: "I think that joint stock banks are deficient in everything requisite for the conduct of the banking business except extended responsibility; the banking business requires peculiarly persons attentive to all its details, constantly, daily, and hourly watchful of every transaction, much more than mercantile or trading business. It also requires immediate prompt decisions upon circumstances when they arise, in many cases a decision that does not admit of delay for consultation; it also requires a discretion to be exercised with reference to the special circumstances of each case. Joint stock banks being of course obliged to act through agents and not by a principal, and therefore under the restraint of general rules, cannot be guided by so nice a reference to degrees of difference in the character of responsibility of parties; nor can they undertake to regulate the assistance to be granted to concerns under temporary embarrassment by so accurate a reference to the circumstances, favourable or unfavourable, of each case."

'But in this very respect, joint stock banks have probably improved the business of banking. The old private banks in former times used to lend much to private individuals; the banker, as Lord Overstone on another occasion explained, could have no security, but he formed his judgment of the discretion, the sense, and the solvency of those to whom he lent. And when London was by comparison a small city, and when by comparison everyone stuck to his proper business, this practice might have been safe. But now that London is enormous and that no one can watch anyone, such a trade would be disastrous; at present, it would hardly be safe in a country town. The joint stock banks were quite unfit for the business Lord Overstone meant, but then that business is quite unfit for the present time.

This success of Joint Stock Banking is very contrary to the general expectation at its origin. Not only private bankers, such as Lord Overstone then was, but a great number of thinking persons feared that the joint stock banks would fast ruin themselves, and then cause a collapse and panic in the country. The whole of English commercial literature between 1830 and 1840 is filled with that idea. Nor did it cease in 1840. So late as 1845, Sir R. Peel thought the foundation of joint stock banks so dangerous that he subjected it to grave and exceptional difficulty. Under the Act of 1845, which he proposed, no such companies could be founded except with shares of 100 L. with 50 L.; paid up on each; which effectually checked the progress of such banks, for few new ones were established for many years, or till that act had been repealed. But in this, as in many other cases, perhaps Sir R. Peel will be found to have been clear-sighted rather than far-sighted. He was afraid of certain joint stock banks which he saw rising around him; but the effect of his legislation was to give to these very banks, if not a monopoly, at any rate an exemption from new rivals. No one now founds or can found a new private bank, and Sir R. Peel by law prevented new joint stock banks from being established. Though he was exceedingly distrustful of the joint stock banks founded between 1826 and 1845, yet in fact he was their especial patron, and he more than any other man encouraged and protected them.

But in this wonderful success there are two dubious points, two considerations of different kinds, which forbid us to say that in other countries, even in countries with the capacity of co-operation, joint stock banks would succeed as well as we have seen that they succeed in England. 1st. These great Banks have not had to keep so large a reserve against their liabilities as it was natural that they should, being of first-rate magnitude, keep. They were at first, of course, very small in comparison with what they are now. They found a number of private bankers grouped round the Bank of England, and they added themselves to the group. Not only did they keep their reserve from the beginning at the Bank of England, but they did not keep so much reserve as they would have kept if there had been no Bank of England. For a long time this was hardly noticed. For many years questions of the 'currency,' particularly questions as to the Act of 1844, engrossed the attention of all who were occupied with these subjects. Even those who were most anxious to speak evil of joint stock banks, did not mention this particular evil. The first time, as far as I know, that it was commented on in any important document, was in an official letter written in 1857 by Mr. Weguelin, who was then Governor of the Bank, to Sir George Lewis, who was then Chancellor of the Exchequer. The Governor and the Directors of the Bank of England had been asked by Sir George Lewis severally to give their opinions on the Act of 1844, and all their replies were published. In his, Mr. Weguelin says:

'If the amount of the reserve kept by the Bank of England be contrasted with the reserve kept by the joint stock banks, a new and hitherto little considered source of danger to the credit of the country will present itself. The joint stock banks of London, judging by their published accounts, have deposits to the amount of 30,000,000 L. Their capital is not more than 3,000,000 L., and they have on an average 31,000,000 L., invested in one way or another, leaving only 2,000,000 L. as a reserve against all this mass of liabilities.'

But these remarkable words were little observed in the discussions of that time. The air was obscured by other matters. But in this work I have said so much on the subject that I need say little now. The joint stock banks now keep a main part of their reserve on deposit with the bill-brokers, or in good and convertible interest-bearing securities. From these they obtain a large income, and that income swells their profits. If they had to keep a much larger part than now of that reserve in barren cash, their dividends would be reduced, and their present success would become less conspicuous.

The second misgiving, which many calm observers more and more feel as to our largest joint stock banks, fastens itself on their government. Is that government sufficient to lend well and keep safe so many millions? They are governed, as every one knows, by a board of directors, assisted by a general manager, and there are in London unrivalled materials for composing good boards of directors. There are very many men of good means, of great sagacity and great experi-ence in business, who are obliged to be in the City every day, and to remain there during the day, but who have very much time on their hands. A merchant employing solely or principally his own capital has often a great deal of leisure. He is obliged to be on the market, and to hear what is doing. Every day he has some business to transact, but his transactions can be but few. His capital can bear only a limited number of purchases; if he bought as much as would fill his time from day to day he would soon be ruined, for he could not pay for it. Accordingly, many excellent men of business are quite ready to become members of boards of directors, and to attend to the business of companies, a good deal for the employment's sake. To have an interesting occupation which brings dignity and power with it pleases them very much. As the aggregation of commerce in great cities grows, the number of such men augments. A council of grave, careful, and experienced men can, without difficulty, be collected for a great bank in London, such as never could have been collected before, and such as cannot now be collected elsewhere.

There are facilities, too, for engaging a good banker to be a manager such as there never were before in the world. The number of such persons is much on the increase. Any careful person who is experienced in figures, and has real sound sense, may easily make himself a good banker. The modes in which money can be safely lent by a banker are not many, and a clear-headed, quiet, industrious person may soon learn all that is necessary about them. Our intricate law of real property is an impediment in country banking, for it requires some special study even

118

to comprehend the elements of a law which is full of technical words, and which can only be explained by narrating its history. But the banking of great cities is little concerned with loans on landed property. And all the rest of the knowledge requisite for a banker can easily be obtained by anyone who has the sort of mind which takes to it. No doubt there is a vast routine of work to be learned, and the manager of a large bank must have a great facility in transacting business rapidly. But a great number of persons are now bred from their earliest manhood in the very midst of that routine; they learn it as they would learn a language, and come to be no more able to unlearn it than they could unlearn a language. And the able ones among them acquire an almost magical rapidity in effecting the business connected with that routine. A very good manager and very good board of directors can, without unreasonable difficulty, be provided for a bank at present in London.

It will be asked, what more can be required? I reply, a great deal. All which the best board of directors can really accomplish, is to form a good decision on the points which the manager presents to them, and perhaps on a few others which one or two zealous members of their body may select for discussion. A meeting of fifteen or eighteen persons is wholly unequal to the transaction of more business than this; it will be fortunate, and it must be well guided, if it should be found to be equal to so much. The discussion even of simple practical points by such a number of persons is a somewhat tedious affair. Many of them will wish to speak on every decision of moment, and some of themsome of the best of them perhapswill only speak with difficulty and slowly. Very generally, several points will be started at once, unless the discussion is strictly watched by a rigid chairman; and even on a single point the arguments will often raise grave questions which cannot be answered, and suggest many more issues than can be advantageously decided by the meeting. The time required by many persons for discussing many questions, would alone prevent an assembly of many persons from overlooking a large and complicated business.

Nor is this the only difficulty. Not only would a real supervision of a large business by a board of directors require much more time than the board would consent to occupy in meeting, it would also require much more time and much more thought than the individual directors would consent to give. These directors are only employing on the business of the Bank the vacant moments of their time, and the spare energies of their minds. They cannot give the Bank more; the rest is required for the safe conduct of their own affairs, and if they diverted it from these affairs they would be ruined. A few of them may have little other business, or they may have other partners in the business, on whose industry they can rely, and whose judgment they can trust; one or two may have retired from business. But for the most part, directors of a company cannot attend principally and anxiously to the affairs of a company without so far neglecting their own business as to run great risk of ruin; and if they are ruined, their trustworthiness ceases, and they are no longer permitted by custom to be directors.

Nor, even if it were possible really to supervise a business by the effectual and constant inspection of fifteen or sixteen rich and capable persons, would even the largest business easily bear the expense of such a supervision. I say rich, because the members of a board governing a large bank must be men of standing and note besides, or they would discredit the bank; they need not be rich in the sense of being worth millions, but they must be known to possess a fair amount of capital and be seen to be transacting a fair quantity of business. But the labour of such persons, I do not say their spare powers, but their principal energies, fetches a high price. Business is really a profession often requiring for its practice quite as much knowledge, and quite as much skill, as law and medicine; and requiring also the possession of money. A thorough man of business, employing a fair capital in a trade, which he thoroughly comprehends, not only earns a profit on that capital, but really makes of his professional skill a large income. He has a revenue from talent as well as from money; and to induce sixteen or eighteen persons to abandon such a position and such an income in order to devote their entire attention to the affairs of a joint stock company, a salary must be given too large for the bank to pay or for anyone to wish to propose.

And an effectual supervision by the whole board being impossible, there is a great risk that the whole business may fall to the general manager. Many unhappy cases have proved this to be very dangerous. Even when the business of joint stock banks was far less, and when the deposits entrusted to them were very much smaller, a manager sometimes committed frauds which were dangerous, and still oftener made mistakes that were ruinous. Actual crime will always be rare; but, as an uninspected manager of a great bank has the control of untold millions, sometimes we must expect to see it: the magnitude of the temptation will occasionally prevail over the feebleness of human nature. But error is far more formidable than fraud: the mistakes of a sanguine manager are, far more to be dreaded than the theft of a dishonest manager. Easy misconception is far more common than long-sighted deceit. And the losses to which an adventurous and plausible manager, in complete good faith, would readily commit a bank, are beyond comparison greater than any which a fraudulent manager would be able to conceal, even with the utmost ingenuity. If the losses by mistake in banking and the losses by fraud were put side by side, those by mistake would be incomparably the greater. There is no more unsafe government for a bank than that of an eager and active manager, subject only to the supervision of a numerous board of directors, even though that board be excellent, for the manager may easily glide into dangerous and insecure transactions, nor can the board effectually check him.

The remedy is this: a certain number of the directors, either those who have more spare time than others, or those who are more ready to sell a large part of their time to the bank, must be formed into a real working committee, which must meet constantly, must investigate every large transaction, must be acquainted with the means and standing of every large borrower, and must be in such incessant communication with the manager that it will be impossible for him to engage in hazardous enterprises of dangerous magnitude without their knowing it and having an opportunity of forbidding it. In almost all cases they would forbid it; all committees are cautious, and a committee of careful men of business, picked from a large city, will usually err on the side of caution if it err at all. The daily attention of a small but competent minor council, to whom most of the powers of the directors are delegated, and who, like a cabinet, guide the deliberations of the board at its meetings, is the only adequate security of a large bank from the rash engagements of a despotic and active general manager. Fraud, in the face of such a committee, would probably never be attempted, and even now it is a rare and minor evil.

Some such committees are vaguely known to exist in most, if not all, our large joint stock banks. But their real constitution is not known. No customer and no shareholder knows the names of the managing committee, perhaps, in any of these large banks. And this is a grave error. A large depositor ought to be able to ascertain who really are the persons that dispose of his money; and still more a large shareholder ought not to rest till he knows who it is that makes engagements on his behalf, and who it is that may ruin him if they choose. The committee ought to be composed of quiet men of business, who can be ascertained by inquiry to be of high character and well-judging mind. And if the public and the shareholder knew that there was such a committee, they would have sufficient reasons for the confidence which now is given without such reasons.

A certain number of directors attending daily by rotation is, it should be said, no substitute for a permanent committee. It has no sufficient responsibility. A changing body cannot have any responsibility. The transactions which were agreed to by one set of directors present on the Monday might be exactly those which would be much disapproved by directors present on the Wednesday. It is essential to the decisions of most business, and not least of the banking business, that they should be made constantly by the same persons; the chain of transactions must pass through the same minds. A large business may be managed tolerably by a quiet group of second-rate men if those men be always the same; but it cannot be managed at all by a fluctuating body, even of the very cleverest men. You might as well attempt to guide the affairs of the nation by means of a cabinet similarly changing.

Our great joint stock bands are imprudent in so carefully concealing the details of their government, and in secluding those details from the risk of discussion. The answer, no doubt will be, 'Let well alone; as you have admitted, there hardly ever before was so great a success as these banks of ours: what more do you or can you want?' I can only say that I want further to confirm this great success and to make it secure for the future. At present there is at least the possibility of a great reaction. Supposing that, owing to defects in its government, one even of the greater London joint stock banks failed, there would be an instant suspicion of the whole system. One terra incognita being seen to be faulty, every other terra incognita would be suspected. If the real government of these banks had for years been known, and if the subsisting banks had been known not to be ruled by the bad mode of government which had ruined the bank that had fallen, then the ruin of that bank would not be hurtful. The other banks would be seen to be exempt from the cause which had destroyed it. But at present the ruin of one of these great banks would greatly impair the credit of all. Scarcely any one knows the precise government of any one; in no case has that government been described on authority; and the fall of one by grave misgovernment would be taken to show that the others might as easily be misgoverned also. And a tardy disclosure even of an admirable constitution would not much help the surviving banks: as it was extracted by necessity, it would be received with suspicion. A sceptical world would say 'of course they say they are all perfect now; it would not do for them to say anything else.'

And not only the depositors and the shareholders of these large banks have a grave interest in their good government, but the public also. We have seen that our banking reserve is, as compared with our liabilities, singularly small; we have seen that the rise of these great banks has lessened the proportion of that reserve to those liabilities; we have seen that the greatest strain on the banking reserve is a 'panic.' Now, no cause is more capable of producing a panic, perhaps none is so capable, as the failure of a first-rate joint stock bank in London. Such an event would have something like the effect of the failure of Overend, Gurney and Co.; scarcely any other event would have an equal effect. And therefore, under the existing constitution of our banking system the government of these great banks is of primary importance to us all.

CHAPTER X.

The Private Banks.

Perhaps some readers of the last part of the last chapter have been inclined to say that I must be a latent enemy to Joint Stock Banking. At any rate, I have pointed out what I think grave defects in it. But I fear that a reader of this chapter may, on like grounds, suppose that I am an enemy to Private Banking. And I can only hope that the two impressions may counteract one another, and may show that I do not intend to be unfair.

I can imagine nothing better in theory or more successful in practice than private banks as they were in the beginning. A man of known wealth, known integrity, and known ability is largely entrusted with the money of his neighbours. The confidence is strictly personal. His neighbours know him, and trust him because they know him. They see daily his manner of life, and judge from it that their confidence is deserved. In rural districts, and in former times, it was difficult for a man to ruin himself except at the place in which he lived; for the most part he spent his money there, and speculated there if he speculated at all. Those who lived there also would soon see if he was acting in a manner to shake their confidence. Even in large cities, as cities then were, it was possible for most persons to ascertain with fair certainty the real position of conspicuous persons, and to learn all which was material in fixing their credit. Accordingly the bankers who for a long series of years passed successfully this strict and continual investigation, became very wealthy and very powerful.

The name 'London Banker' had especially a charmed value. He was supposed to represent, and often did represent, a certain union of pecuniary sagacity and educated refinement which was scarcely to be found in any other part of society. In a time when the trading classes were much ruder than they now are, many private bankers possessed variety of knowledge and a delicacy of attainment which would even now be very rare. Such a position is indeed singularly favourable. The calling is hereditary; the credit of the bank descends from father to son: this inherited wealth soon begins inherited refinement. Banking is a watchful, but not a laborious trade. A banker, even in large business, can feel pretty sure that all his transactions are sound, and yet have much spare mind. A certain part of his time, and a considerable part of his thoughts, he can readily devote to other pursuits. And a London banker can also have the most intellectual society in the world if he chooses it. There has probably very rarely ever been so happy a position as that of a London private banker; and never perhaps a happier.

It is painful to have to doubt of the continuance of such a class, and yet, I fear, we must doubt of it. The evidence of figures is against it. In 1810 there were 40 private banks in Lombard Street admitted to the clearing-house: there now are only 3. Though the business of banking has increased so much since 1810, this species of banks is fewer in number than it was then. Nor is this the worst. The race is not renewed. There are not many recognised impossibilities in business, but everybody admits 'that you cannot found a new private bank.' No such has been founded in London, or, as far as I know, in the country, for many years. The old ones merge or die, and so the number is lessened; but no new ones begin so as to increase that number again.

The truth is that the circumstances which originally favoured the establishment of private banks have now almost passed away. The world has become so large and complicated that it is not easy to ascertain who is rich and who is poor. No doubt there are some enormously wealthy men in England whose means everybody has heard of, and has no doubt of. But these are not the men to incur the vast liabilities of private banking. If they were bred in it they might stay in it; but they would never begin it for themselves. And if they did, I expect people would begin to doubt even of their wealth. It would be said, 'What does A B go into banking for? he cannot be as rich as we thought.' A millionaire commonly shrinks from liability, and the essence of great banking is great liability. No doubt there are many 'second-rate' rich men, as we now count riches, who would be quite ready to add to their income the profit of a private bank if only they could manage it. But unluckily they cannot manage it. Their wealth is not sufficiently familiar to the world; they cannot obtain the necessary confidence. No new private bank is founded in England because men of first-rate wealth will not found one, and men not of absolutely first-rate wealth cannot.

In the present day, also, private banking is exposed to a competition against which in its origin it had not to struggle. Owing to the changes of which I have before spoken, joint stock banking has begun to compete with it. In old times this was impossible; the Bank of England had a monopoly in banking of the principle of association. But now large joint stock banks of deposit are among the most conspicuous banks in Lombard Street. They have a large paid-up capital and intelligible published accounts; they use these as an incessant advertisement, in a manner in which no individual can use his own wealth. By their increasing progress they effectually prevent the foundation of any new private bank.

The amount of the present business of private banks is perfectly unknown. Their balance sheets are effective secretsrigidly guarded. But none of them, except a few of the largest, are believed at all to gain business. The common repute of Lombard Street might be wrong in a particular case, but upon the general doctrine it is almost sure to be right. There are a few well-known exceptions, but according to universal belief the deposits of most private bankers in London tend rather to diminish than to increase.

As to the smaller banks, this naturally would be so. A large bank always tends to become larger, and a small one tends to become smaller. People naturally choose for their banker the banker who has most present credit, and the one who has most money in hand is the one who possesses such credit. This is what is meant by saying that a long established and rich bank has a 'privileged opportunity'; it is in a better position to do its business than any one else is; it has a great advantage over old competitors and an overwhelming superiority over new comers. New people coming into Lombard Street judge by results; they give to those who have: they take their money to the biggest bank because it is the biggest. I confess I cannot, looking far forward into the future, expect that the smaller private banks will maintain their ground. Their old connections will not leave them; there will be no fatal ruin, no sudden mortality. But the tide will gently ebb, and the course of business will be carried elsewhere.

Sooner or later, appearances indicate, and principle suggests, that the business of Lombard Street will be divided between the joint stock banks and a few large private banks. And then we have to ask ourserves the question, can those large private banks be permanent? I am sure I should be very sorry to say that they certainly cannot, but at the same time I cannot be blind to the grave difficulties which they must surmount.

In the first place, an hereditary business of great magnitude is dangerous. The management of such a business needs more than common industry and more than common ability. But there is no security at all that these will be regularly continued in each generation. The case of Overend, Gurney and Co., the model instance of all evil in business, is a most alarming example of this evil. No cleverer men of business probably (cleverer I mean for the purposes of their particular calling) could well be found than the founders and first managers of that house. But in a very few years the rule in it passed to a generation whose folly surpassed the usual limit of imaginable incapacity. In a short time they substituted ruin for prosperity and changed opulence into insolvency. Such great folly is happily rare; and the business of a bank is not nearly as difficult as the business of a discount company. Still much folly is common, and the business of a great bank requires a great deal of ability, and an even rarer degree of trained and sober judgment. That which happened so marvelously in the green tree may happen also in the dry. A great private bank might easily become very rotten by a change from discretion to foolishness in those who conduct it.

We have had as yet in London, happily, no example of this; indeed, we have hardly as yet had the opportunity. Till now private banks have been small; small as we now reckon banks. For their exigencies a moderate degree of ability and an anxious caution will suffice. But if the size of the banks is augmented and greater ability is required, the constant difficulty of an hereditary government will begin to be felt. 'The father had great brains and created the business: but the son had less brains and lost or lessened it.' This is the history of all great monarchies, and it may be the history of great private banks. The peculiarity in the case of Overend, Gurney and Co. at least, one peculiarity is that the evil was soon discovered. The richest partners had least concern in the management; and when they found that incredible losses were ruining them, they stopped the concern and turned it into a company. But they had done nothing; if at least they had only prevented farther losses, the firm might have been in existence and in the highest credit now. It was the publicity of their losses which ruined them. But if they had continued to be a private partnership they need not have disclosed those losses: they might have written them off quietly out of the immense profits they could have accumulated. They had some ten millions of other people's money in their hands which no one thought of disturbing. The perturbation through the country which their failure caused in the end, shows how diffused and how unimpaired their popular reputation was. No one in the rural districts (as I know by experience) would ever believe a word against them, say what you might. The catastrophe came because at the change the partners in the old private firmthe Gurney family especiallyhad guaranteed the new company against the previous losses: those losses turned out to be much greater than was expected. To pay what was necessary the 'Gurneys' had to sell their estates, and their visible ruin destroyed the credit of the concern. But if there had been no such guarantee, and no sale of estates, if the great losses had slept a quiet sleep in a hidden ledger, no one would have been alarmed, and the credit and the business of 'Overends' might have existed till now, and their name still continued to be one of our first names. The difficulty of propagating a good management by inheritance for generations is greatest in private banks and discount firms because of their essential secrecy.

The danger may indeed be surmounted by the continual infusion of new and able partners. The deterioration of the old blood may be compensated by the excellent quality of the fresh blood. But to this again there is an objection, of little value perhaps in seeming, but of much real influence in practice. The infusion of new partners requires from the old partners a considerable sacrifice of income; the old must give up that which the new receive, and the old will not like this. The effectual remedy is so painful that I fear it often may be postponed too long.

I cannot, therefore, expect with certainty the continuance of our system of private banking. I am sure that the days of small banks will before many years come to an end, and that the difficulties of large private banks are very important. In the mean time it is very important that large private banks should be well managed. And the present state of banking makes this peculiarly difficult. The detail of the business is augmenting with an overwhelming rapidity. More cheques are drawn year by year; not only more absolutely, but more by each person, and more in proportion to his income. The payments in, and payments out of a common account are very much more numerous than they formerly were. And this causes an enormous growth of detail. And besides, bankers have of late begun almost a new business. They now not only keep people's money, but also collect their incomes for them. Many persons live entirely on the income of shares, or debentures, or foreign bonds, which is paid in coupons, and these are handed in for the bank to collect. Often enough the debenture, or the certificate, or the bond is in the custody of the banker, and he is expected to see when the coupon is due, and to cut it off and transmit it for payment. And the detail of all this is incredible, and it needs a special machinery to cope with it.

A large joint stock bank, if well-worked, has that machinery. It has at the head of the executive a general manager who was tried in the detail of banking, who is devoted to it, and who is content to live almost wholly in it. He thinks of little else, and ought to think of little else. One of his first duties is to form a hierarchy of inferior officers, whose respective duties are defined, and to see that they can perform and do perform those duties. But a private bank of the type usual in London has no such officer. It is managed by the partners; now these are generally rich men, are seldom able to grapple with great business of detail, and are not disposed to spend their whole lives and devote their entire minds to it if they were able. A person with the accumulated wealth, the education and the social place of a great London banker would be a 'fool so to devote himself. He would sacrifice a suitable and a pleasant life for an unpleasant and an unsuitable life. But still the detail must be well done; and some one must be specially chosen to watch it and to preside over it, or it will not be well done. Until now, or until lately, this difficulty has not been fully felt. The detail of the business of a small private bank was moderate enough to be superintended effectually by the partners. But, as has been said, the detail of bankingthe proportion of detail to the size of the bankis everywhere increasing. The size of the private banks will have to augment if private banks are not to cease; and therefore the necessity of a good organisation for detail is urgent. If the bank grows, and simultaneously the detail grows in proportion to the bank, a frightful confusion is near unless care be taken.

The only organisation which I can imagine to be effectual is that which exists in the antagonistic establishments. The great private banks will have, I believe, to appoint in some form or other, and under some name or other, some species of general manager who will watch, contrive, and arrange the detail for them. The precise shape of the organisation is immaterial; each bank may have its own shape, but the man must be there. The true business of the private partners in such a bank is much that of the directors in a joint stock bank. They should form a permanent committee to consult with their general manager, to watch him, and to attend to large loans and points of principle. They should not themselves be responsible for detail; if they do there will be two evils at once: the detail will be done badly, and the minds of those who ought to decide principal things will be distracted from those principal things. There will be a continual worry in the bank, and in a worry bad loans are apt to be made and money is apt to be lost.

A subsidiary advantage of this organisation is that it would render the transition from private banking to joint stock banking easier, if that transition should be necessary. The one might merge in the other as convenience suggested and as events required. There is nothing intrusive in discussing this subject. The organisation of the private is just like that of the joint stock banks; all the public are interested that it should be good. The want of a good organisation may cause the failure of one or more of these banks; and such failure of such banks may intensify a panic, even if it should not cause one.

CHAPTER XI.

The Bill-Brokers.

Under every system of banking, whether that in which the reserve is kept in many banks, or one in which it is kept in a single bank only, there will always be a class of persons who examine more carefully than busy bankers can the nature of different securities; and who, by attending only to one class, come to be particularly well acquainted with that class. And as these specially qualified dealers can for the most part lend much more than their own capital, they will always be ready to borrow largely from bankers and others, and to deposit the securities which they know to be good as a pledge for the loan. They act thus as intermediaries between the borrowing public and the less qualified capitalist; knowing better than the ordinary capitalist which loans are better and which are worse, they borrow from him, and gain a profit by charging to the public more than they pay to him.

Many stock brokers transact such business upon a great scale. They lend large sums on foreign bonds or railway shares or other such securities, and borrow those sums from bankers, depositing the securities with the bankers, and generally, though not always, giving their guarantee. But by far the greatest of these intermediate dealers are the bill-brokers. Mercantile bills are an exceedingly difficult kind of security to understand. The relative credit of different merchants is a great 'tradition'; it is a large mass of most valuable knowledge which has never been described in books and is probably incapable of being so described. The subject matter of it, too, is shifting and changing daily; an accurate representation of the trustworthiness of houses at the beginning of a year might easily be a most fatal representation at the end of it. In all years there are great changes; some houses rise a good deal and some fall. And in some particular years the changes are immense; in years like 1871 many active men make so much money that at the end of the year they are worthy of altogether greater credit than anyone would have dreamed of giving to them at the beginning.

On the other hand, in years like 1866 a contagious ruin destroys the trustworthiness of very many firms and persons, and often, especially, of many who stood highest immediately before. Such years alter altogether an important part of the mercantile world: the final question of bill-brokers, 'which bills will be paid and which will not? which bills are second-rate and which first-rate?' would be answered very differently at the beginning of the year and at the end. No one can be a good bill-broker who has not learnt the great mercantile tradition of what is called 'the standing of parties' and who does not watch personally and incessantly the inevitable changes which from hour to hour impair the truth of that tradition. The credit' of a personthat is, the reliance which may be placed on his pecuniary fidelityis a different thing from his property. No doubt, other things being equal, a rich man is more likely to pay than a poor man. But on the other hand, there are many men not of much wealth who are trusted in the market, 'as a matter of business,' for sums much exceeding the wealth of those who are many times richer. A firm or a person who have been long known to 'meet their engagements,' inspire a degree of confidence not dependent on the quantity of his or their property. Persons who buy to sell again soon are often liable for amounts altogether much greater than their own capital; and the power of obtaining those sums depends upon their 'respectability,' their 'standing,' and their 'credit,' as the technical terms express it, and more simply upon the opinion which those who deal with them have formed of them. The principal mode in which money is raised by traders is by 'bills of exchange;' the estimated certainty of their paying those bills on the day they fall due is the measure of their credit; and those who estimate that liability best, the only persons indeed who can estimate it exceedingly well, are the bill-brokers. And these dealers, taking advantage of their peculiar knowledge, borrow immense sums from bankers and others; they generally deposit the bills as a security; and they generally give their own guarantee of the goodness of the bill: but neither of such practices indeed is essential, though both are the ordinary rule. When Overends failed, as I have said before, they had borrowed in this way very largely. There are others now in the trade who have borrowed quite as much.

As is usually the case, this kind of business has grown up only gradually. In the year 1810 there was no such business precisely answering to what we now call bill-broking in London. Mr. Richardson, the principal 'bill-broker' of the time, as the term was then understood, thus described his business to the 'Bullion Committee:'

'What is the nature of the agency for country banks'It is twofold: in the first place to procure money for country bankers on bills when they have occasion to borrow on discount, which is not often the case; and in the next place, to lend the money for the country bankers on bills on discount. The sums of money which I lend for country bankers on discount are fifty times more than the sums borrowed for country bankers.

'Do you send London bills into the country for discount?--Yes.

'Do you receive bills from the country upon London in return, at a date, to be discounted?--Yes, to a very considerable amount, from particular parts of the country.

'Are not both sets of bills by this means under discount?--No, the bills received from one part of the country are sent down to another part for discount.

'And they are not discounted in London?--No. In some parts of the country there is but little circulation of bills drawn upon London, as in Norfolk, Suffolk, Essex, Sussex, &c.; but there is there a considerable circulation in country bank-notes, principally optional notes. In Lancashire there is little or no circulation of country bank-notes; but there is a great circulation of bills drawn upon London at two or three months' date. I receive bills to a considerable amount from Lancashire in particular, and remit them to Norfolk, Suffolk, &c., where the bankers have large lodgments, and much surplus money to advance on bills for discount.'

Mr. Richardson was only a broker who found money for bills and bills for money. He is further asked:

'Do you guarantee the bills you discount, and what is your charge per cent?--No, we do not guarantee them; our charge is one-eighth per cent brokerage upon the bill discounted, but we make no charge to the lender of the money.

'Do you consider that brokerage as a compensation for the skill which you exercise in selecting the bills which you thus get discounted?--Yes, for selecting of the bills, writing letters, and other trouble.

'Does the party who furnishes the money give you any kind of compensation?--None at all.

'Does he not consider you as his agent, and in some degree responsible for the safety of the bills which you give him?--Not at all.

'Does he not prefer you on the score of his judging that you will give him good intelligence upon that subject?--Yes, he relies upon us.

'Do you then exercise a discretion as to the probable safety of the bills?--Yes; if a bill comes to us which we conceive not to be safe, we return it.

'Do you not then conceive yourselves to depend in a great measure for the quantity of business which you can perform on the favour of the party lending the money?--Yes, very much so. If we manage our business well, we retain our friends; if we do not, we lose them.'

131

It was natural enough that the owners of the money should not pay, though the owner of the bill did, for in almost all ages the borrower has been a seeker more or less anxious; he has always been ready to pay for those who will find him the money he is in search of. But the possessor of money has rarely been willing to pay anything; he has usually and rightly believed that the borrower would discover him soon.

Notwithstanding other changes, the distribution of the customers of the bill-brokers in different parts of the country still remains much as Mr. Richardson described it sixty years ago. For the most part, agricultural counties do not employ as much money as they save; manufacturing counties, on the other hand, can employ much more than they save; and therefore the money of Norfolk or of Somersetshire is deposited with the London bill-brokers, who use it to discount the bills of Lancashire and Yorkshire.

The old practice of bill-broking, which Mr. Richardson describes, also still exists. There are many brokers to be seen about Lombard Street with bills which they wish to discount but which they do not guarantee. They have sometimes discounted these bills with their own capital, and if they can re-discount them at a slightly lower rate they gain a difference which at first seems but trifling, but with which they are quite content, because this system of lending first and borrowing again immediately enables them to turn their capital very frequently, and on a few thousand pounds of capital to discount hundreds of thousands of bills; as the transactions are so many, they can be content with a smaller profit on each. In other cases, these nonguaranteeing brokers are only agents who are seeking money for bills which they have undertaken to get discounted. But in either case, as far as the banker or other ultimate capitalist is concerned, the transaction is essentially that which Mr. Richardson describes. The loan by such banker is a rediscount of the bill; that banker cannot obtain repayment of that loan, except by the payment of the bill at maturity. He has no claim upon the agent who brought him the bill. Billbroking, in this which we may call its archaic form, is simply one of the modes in which bankers obtain bills which are acceptable to them and which they rediscount. No reference is made in it to the credit of the bill-broker; the bills being discounted 'without recourse' to him are as good if taken from a pauper as if taken from a millionaire. The lender exercises his own judgment on the goodness of the bill.

But in modern bill-broking the credit of the bill-broker is a vital element. The lender considers that the bill-brokerno matter whether an individual, a company, or a firmhas considerable wealth, and he takes the 'bills,' relying that the broker would not venture that wealth by guaranteeing them unless he thought them good. The lender thinks, too, that the bill-broker being daily conversant with bills and bills only, knows probably all about bills: he lends partly in reliance on the wealth of the broker and partly in reliance on his skill. He does not exercise much judgment of his own on the bills deposited with him: he often does not watch them very closely. Probably not one-thousandth part of the creditors on security of Overend, Gurney and Co., had ever expected to have to rely on that security, or had ever given much real attention to it. Sometimes, indeed, the confidence in the bill-brokers goes farther. A considerable number of persons lend to them, not only without much looking at the security but even without taking any security. This is the exact reverse of the practice which Mr. Richardson described in 1810; then the lender relied wholly on the goodness of the bill, now, in these particular cases, he relies solely on the bill-broker, and does not take a bill in any shape. Nothing can be more natural or more inevitable than this change. It was certain that the bill-broker, being supposed to understand bills well, would be asked by the lenders to evince his reliance on the bills he offered by giving a guarantee for them. It was also most natural that the bill-brokers, having by the constant practice of this lucrative trade obtained high standing and acquired great wealth, should become, more or less, bankers too, and should receive money on deposit without giving any security for it.

But the effects of the change have been very remarkable. In the practice as Mr. Richardson described it, there is no peculiarity very likely to affect the money market. The bill-broker brought bills to the banker, just as others brought them; nothing at all could be said as to it except that the Bank must not discount bad bills, must not discount too many bills, and must keep a good reserve. But the modern practice introduces more complex considerations. In the trade of bill-broking, as it now exists, there is one great difficulty; the bill-broker has to pay interest for all the money which he receives. How this arose we have just seen. The present lender to the bill-broker at first always used to discount a bill, which is as much as saying that he was always a lender at interest. When he came to take the guarantee of the broker, and only to look at the bills as a collateral security, naturally he did not forego his interest: still less did he forego it when he ceased to take security at all. The bill-broker has, in one shape or other, to pay interest on every sixpence left with him, and that constant habit of giving interest has this grave consequence: the bill-broker cannot afford to keep much money unemployed. He has become a banker owing large sums which he may be called on to repay, but he cannot hold as much as an ordinary banker, or nearly as much, of such sums in cash, because the loss of interest would ruin him. Competition reduces the rate which the bill-broker can charge, and raises the rate which the bill-broker must give, so that he has to live on a difference exceedingly narrow. And if he constantly kept a large hoard of barren money he would soon be found in the 'Gazette.'

The difficulty is aggravated by the terms upon which a great part of the money at the bill-brokers is deposited with them. Very much of it is repayable at demand, or at very short notice. The demands on a broker in periods of alarm may consequently be very great, and in practice they often, are so. In times of panic there is always a very heavy call, if not a run upon them; and in consequence of the essential nature of their business, they cannot constantly keep a large unemployed reserve of their own in actual cash, they are obliged to ask help of some one who possesses that cash. By the conditions of his trade, the bill-broker is forced to belong to a class of 'dependent money-dealers,' as we may term them, that is, of dealers who do not keep their own reserve, and must, therefore, at every crisis of great difficulty revert to others.

In a natural state of banking, that in which all the principal banks kept their own reserve, this demand of the bill-brokers and other dependent dealers would be one of the principal calls on that reserve. At every period of incipient panic the holders of it would perceive that it was of great importance to themselves to support these dependent dealers. If the panic destroyed those dealers it would grow by what it fed upon (as is its nature), and might probably destroy also the bankers, the holders of the reserve. The public terror at such times is indiscriminate. When one house of good credit has perished, other houses of equal credit though of different nature are m danger of perishing. The many holders of the banking reserve would under the natural system of banking be obliged to advance out of that reserve to uphold bill-brokers and similar dealers. It would be essential to their own preservation not to let such dealers fail, and the protection of such dealers would therefore be reckoned among the necessary purposes for which they retained that reserve.

Nor probably would the demands on the bill-brokers in such a system of banking be exceedingly formidable. Considerable sums would no doubt be drawn from them, but there would be no special reason why money should be demanded from them more than from any other money dealers. They would share the panic with the bankers who kept the reserve, but they would not feel it more than the bankers. In each crisis the set of the storm would be determined by the cause which had excited it, but there would not be anything in the nature of bill-broking to attract the advance of the alarm peculiarly to them. They would not be more likely to suffer than other persons; the only difference would be that when they did suffer, having no adequate reserve of their own, they would be obliged to ask the aid of others.

But under a one-reserve system of banking, the position of the bill-brokers is much more singular and much more precarious. In fact, in Lombard Street, the principal depositors of the bill-brokers are the bankers, whether of London, or of provincial England, or of Scotland, or Ireland. Such deposits are, in fact, a portion of the reserve of these bankers; they make an essential part of the sums which they have provided and laid by against a panic. Accordingly, in every panic these sums are sure to be called in from the bill-brokers; they were wanted to be used by their owners in time of panic, and in time of panic they ask for them. 'Perhaps it may be interesting,' said Alderman Salomons, speaking on behalf of the London and Westminster Bank, after the panic of 1857, to the committee, 'to know that, on November 11, we held discounted bills for brokers to the amount of 5,623,000 L. Out of these bills 2,800,000 L. matured between November 1 and December 4; 2,000,000 L. more between December 1 and December 31; consequently we were prepared merely by the maturing of our bills of exchange for any demand that might come upon us.' This is not indeed a direct withdrawal of money on deposit, but its principal effect is identical. At the beginning of the time the London and Westminster Bank had lent 5,000,000 L. more to the bill-brokers than they had at the end of it; and that 5,000,000 L. the bank had added to its reserve against a time of difficulty.

The intensity of the demand on the bill-broker is aggravated therefore by our peculiar system of banking. Just at the moment when, by the nature of their business, they have to resort to the reserves of bankers for necessary support, the bankers remove from them large sums in order to strengthen those reserves. A great additional strain is thrown upon them just at the moment when they are least able to bear it; and it is thrown by those who under a natural system of banking would not aggravate the pressure on the bill-brokers, but relieve it.

And the profits of bill-broking are proportionably raised. The reserves of the bankers so deposited with the bill-broker form a most profitable part of his business; they are on the whole of very large amount, and at all times, except those of panic, may well be depended upon. The bankers are pretty sure to keep them there, just because they must keep a reserve, and they consider it one of the best places in which to keep it. Under a more natural system, no part of the banking reserve would ever be lodged at the brokers. Bankers would deposit with the brokers only their extra money, the money which they considered they could safely lend, and which they would not require during a panic. In the eye of the banker, money at the brokers would then be one of the investments of cash, it would not be a part of such cash. The deposits of bill-brokers and the profits of bill-broking are increased by our present system, just in proportion as the dangers of bill-brokers during a panic are increased by it.

The strain, too, on our banking reserve which is caused by the demands of the bill-brokers, is also more dangerous than it would be under a natural system, because that reserve is in itself less. The system of keeping the entire ultimate reserve at a single bank, undoubtedly diminishes the amount of reserve which is kept. And exactly on that very account the danger of any particular demand on that reserve is augmented, because the magnitude of the fund upon which that demand falls is diminished. So that our one-reserve system of banking combines two evils: first, it makes the demand of the brokers upon the final reserve greater, because under it so many bankers remove so much money from the brokers; and under it also the final reserve is reduced to its minimum point, and the entire system of credit is made more delicate, and more sensitive.

135

The peculiarity, indeed, of the effects of the one reserve is indeed even greater in this respect. Under the natural system, the billbrokers would be in no respect the rivals of the bankers which kept the ultimate reserve. They would be rather the agents for these bankers in lending upon certain securities which they did not themselves like, or on which they did not feel competent to lend safely. The bankers who in time of panic had to help them would in ordinary times derive much advantage from them. But under our present system all this is reversed. The Bank of England never deposits any money with the bill-brokers; in ordinary times it never derives any advantage from them. On the other hand, as the Bank carries on itself a large discount business, as it considers that it is itself competent to lend on all kinds of bills, the bill-brokers are its most formidable rivals. As they constantly give high rates for money it is necessary that they should undersell the Bank, and in ordinary times they do undersell it. But as the Bank of England alone keeps the final banking reserve, the bill-brokers of necessity have to resort to that final reserve; so that at every panic, and by the essential constitution of the money market, the Bank of England has to help, has to maintain in existence, the dealers, who never in return help the Bank at any time, but who are in ordinary times its closest competitors and its keenest rivals.

It might be expected that such a state of things would cause much discontent at the Bank of England, and in matter of fact there has been much discussion about it, and much objection taken to it. After the panic of 1857, this was so especially. During that panic, the Bank of England advanced to the bill-brokers more than 9,000,000 L., though their advances to bankers, whether London or country, were only 8,000,000 L.; and, not unnaturally, the Bank thought it unreasonable that so large an inroad upon their resources should be made by their rivals. In consequence, in 1858 they made a rule that they would only advance to the bill-brokers at certain seasons of the year, when the public money is particularly large at the bank, and that at other times any application for an advance should be considered excep tonal, and dealt with accordingly. And the object of that regulation was officially stated to be 'to make them keep their own reserve, and not to be dependent on the Bank of England.' As might be supposed, this rule was exceedingly unpopular with the brokers, and the greatest of them, Overend, Gurney and Co., resolved on a strange policy in the hope of abolishing it. They thought they could frighten the Bank of England, and could show that if they were dependent on it, it was also dependent on them. They accordingly accumulated a large deposit at the Bank to the amount of 3,000,000 L., and then withdrew it all at once. But this policy had no effect, except that of exciting a distrust of 'Overends': the credit of the Bank of England was not diminished; Overends had to return the money in a few days, and had the dissatisfaction of feeling that they had in vain attempted to assail the solid basis of everyone's credit, and that everyone disliked them for doing so. But though this un-conceived attempt failed as it deserved, the rule itself could not be maintained. The Bank does, in fact, at every period of pressure, advance to the bin-brokers; the case may be considered 'exceptional,' but the advance is always made if the security offered is really good. However much the Bank may dislike to aid their rivals, yet they must aid them; at a crisis they feel that they would only be aggravating incipient demand, and be augmenting the probable pressure on themselves if they refused to do so.

I shall be asked if this anomaly is inevitable, and I am afraid that for practical purposes we must consider it to be so. It may be lessened; the bill-brokers may, and should, discourage as much as they can the deposit of money with them on demand, and encourage the deposit of it at distant fixed dates or long notice. This will diminish the anomaly, but it will not cure it. Practically, bin-brokers cannot refuse to receive money at call. In every market a dealer must conduct his business according to the custom of the market, or he will not be able to conduct it at all. All the bin-brokers can do is to offer better rates for more permanent money, and this (though possibly not so much as might be wished) they do at present. In its essence, this anomaly is, I believe, an inevitable part of the system of banking which history has given us, and which we have only to make the best of, since we cannot alter it.

CHAPTER XII.

The Principles Which Should Regulate the Amount of the Banking Reserve to Be Kept by the Bank of England.

There is a very common notion that the amount of the reserve which the Bank of England ought to keep can be determined at once from the face of their weekly balance sheet. It is imagined that you have only to take the liabilities of the Banking department, and that a third or some other fixed proportion will in all cases be the amount of reserve which the Bank should keep against those liabilities. But to this there are several objections, some arising from the general nature of the banking trade, and others from the special position of the Bank of England.

That the amount of the liabilities of a bank is a principal element in determining the proper amount of its reserve is plainly true; but that it is the only element by which that amount is determined is plainly false. The intrinsic nature of these liabilities must be considered, as well as their numerical quantity. For example, no one would say that the same amount of reserve ought to be kept against acceptances which cannot be paid except at a certain day, and against deposits at call, which may be demanded at any moment. If a bank groups these liabilities together in the balance-sheet, you cannot tell the amount of reserve it ought to keep. The necessary information is not given you.

Nor can you certainly determine the amount of reserve necessary to be kept against deposits unless you know something as to the nature of these deposits. If out of 3,000,000 L. of money, one depositor has 1,000,000 L. to his credit, and may draw it out when he pleases, a much larger reserve will be necessary against that liability of 1,000,000 L. than against the remaining 2,000,000 L. The intensity of the liability, so to say, is much greater; and therefore the provision in store must be much greater also. On the other hand, supposing that this single depositor is one of calculable habitssuppose that it is a public body, the time of whose demands is known, and the time of whose receipts is known alsothis single liability requires a less reserve than that of an equal amount of ordinary liabilities. The danger that it win be called for is much less; and therefore the security taken against it may be much less too. Unless the quality of the liabilities is considered as well as their quantity, the due provision for their payment cannot be determined.

These are general truths as to all banks, and they have a very particular application to the Bank of England. The first application is favourable to the Bank; for it shows the danger of one of the principal liabilities to be much smaller than it seems. The largest account at the Bank of England is that of the English Government; and probably there has never been any account of which it was so easy in time of peace to calculate the course. All the material facts relative to the English revenue, and the English expenditure, are exceedingly well known; and the amount of the coming payments to and from this account are always, except in war times, to be calculated with wonderful accuracy. In war, no doubt, this is all reversed; the account of a government at war is probably the most uncertain of all accounts, especially of a government of a scattered empire, like the English, whose places of outlay in time of war are so many and so distant, and the amount of whose payments is therefore so incalculable. Ordinarily, however, there is no account of which the course can be so easily predicted; and therefore no account which needs in ordinary times so little reserve. The principal payments, when they are made, are also of the most satisfactory kind to a banker; they are, to a great extent, made to another account at his bank. These largest ordinary payments of the Government are the dividends on the debt, and these are mostly made to bankers who act as agents for the creditors of the nation. The payment of the dividends for the Government is, therefore, in great part a transfer from the account of the Government to the accounts of the various bankers. A certain amount no doubt goes almost at once to the non-banking classes; to those who keep coin and notes in house, and have no account at any bank. But even this amount is calculable, for it is always nearly the same. And the entire operation is, to those who can watch it, singularly invariable time after time.

But it is important to observe, that the published accounts of the Bank give no such information to the public as win enable them to make their own calculations. The account of which we have been speaking is the yearly account of the English Governmentwhat we may call the Budget account, that of revenue and expenditure. And the laws of this are, as we have shown, already known. But under the head 'Public Deposits' in the accounts of the Bank, are contained also other accounts, and particularly that of the Secretary for India in Council, the laws of which must be different and are quite unknown. The Secretary for India is a large lender on its account. If any one proposed to give such power to the Chancellor of the Exchequer, there would be great fear and outcry. But so much depends on habit and tradition, that the India Office on one side of Downing Street can do without remark, and with universal assent, what it would be thought 'unsound' and extravagant to propose that the other side should do. The present India Office inherits this independence from the old Board of the Company, which, being mercantile and business-like, used to lend its own money on the Stock Exchange as it pleased; the Council of India, its successor, retains the power. Nothing can be better than that it should be allowed to do as it likes; but the mixing up the account of a body which has such a power, and which draws money from India, with that of the Home government clearly prevents the general public from being able to draw inferences as to the course of the combined account from its knowledge of home finance only. The account of 'public deposits' in the Bank return includes other accounts too, as the Savings' Bank balance, the Chancery Funds account, and others; and in consequence, till lately the public had but little knowledge of the real changes of the account of our Government, properly so called. But Mr. Lowe has lately given us a weekly account, and from this, and not from the Bank account, we are able to form a judgment. This account and the return of the Bank of England, it is true, unhappily appear on different days; but except for that accident our knowledge would be perfect; and as it is, for almost all purposes what we know is reasonably sufficient. We can now calculate the course of the Government account nearly as well as it is possible to calculate it.

So far, as we have said, an analysis of the return of the Bank of England is very favourable to the Bank. So great a reserve need not usually be kept against the Government account as if it were a common account. We know the laws of its changes peculiarly well: we can tell when its principal changes will happen with great accuracy; and we know that at such changes most of what is paid away by the Government is only paid to other depositors at the Bank, and that it win really stay at the Bank, though under another name. If we look to the private deposits of the Bank of England, at first sight we may think that the result is the same. By far the most important of these are the 'Bankers' deposits'; and, for the most part, these deposits as a whole are likely to vary very little. Each banker, we will suppose, keeps as little as he can, but in all domestic transactions payment from one is really payment to the other. All the most important transactions in the country are settled by cheques; these cheques are paid in to the 'clearing-house,' and the balances resulting from them are settled by transfers from the account of one banker to another at the Bank of England. Payments out of the bankers' balances, therefore, correspond with payments in. As a whole, the deposit of the bankers' balances at the Bank of England would at first sight seem to be a deposit singularly stable.

Indeed, they would seem, so to say, to be better than stable. They augment when everything else tends to diminish. At a panic, when all other deposits are likely to be taken away, the bankers' deposits, augment; in fact they did so in 1866, though we do not know the particulars; and it is natural that they should so increase. At such moments all bankers are extremely anxious, and they try to strengthen themselves by every means in their power; they try to have as much money as it is possible at command; they augment their reserve as much as they can, and they place that reserve at the Bank of England. A deposit which is not likely to vary in ordinary times, and which is likely to augment in times of danger, seems, in some sort, the model of a deposit. It might seem not only that a large proportion of it might be lent, but that the whole of it might be so. But a further analysis will, as I believe, show that this conclusion is entirely false; that the bankers' deposits are a singularly treacherous form of liability; that the utmost caution ought to be used in dealing with them; that, as a rule, a less proportion of them ought to be lent than of ordinary deposits.

The easiest mode of explaining anything is, usually, to exemplify it by a single actual case. And in this subject, fortunately, there is a most conspicuous case near at hand. The German Government has lately taken large sums in bullion from this country, in part from the Bank of England, and in part not, according as it chose. It was in the main well advised, and considerate in its action; and did not take nearly as much from the Bank as it might, or as would have been dangerous. Still it took large sums from the Bank; and it might easily have taken more. How then did the German Government obtain this vast power over the Bank? The answer is, that it obtained it by means of the bankers' balances, and that it did so in two ways.

First, the German Government had a large balance of its own lying at a particular Joint Stock Bank. That bank lent this balance at its own discretion, to bill-brokers or others, and it formed a single item in the general funds of the London market. There was nothing special about it, except that it belonged to a foreign government, and that its owner was always likely to call it in, and sometimes did so. As long as it stayed unlent in the London Joint Stock Bank, it increased the balances of that bank at the Bank of England; but so soon as it was lent, say, to a bill-broker, it increased the bill-broker's balance; and as soon as it was employed by the bill-broker in the discount of bills, the owners of those bills paid it to their credit at their separate banks, and it augmented the balances of those bankers at the Bank of England. Of course if it were employed in the discount of bills belonging to foreigners, the money might be taken abroad, and by similar operations it might also be transferred to the English provinces or to Scotland. But, as a rule, such money when deposited in London, for a considerable time remains in London; and so long as it does so, it swells the aggregate balances of the body of bankers at the Bank of England. It is now in the balance of one bank, now of another, but it is always dispersed about those balances somewhere. The evident consequence is that this part of the bankers' balances is at the mercy of the German Government when it chooses to apply for it. Supposing, then, the sum to be three or four millions and I believe that on more than one occasion in the last year or two it has been quite as much, if not more--that sum might at once be withdrawn from the Bank of England. In this case the Bank of England is in the position of a banker who is liable for a large amount to a single customer, but with this addition, that it is liable for an unknown amount.

The German Government, as is well known, keeps its account (and a very valuable one it must be) at the London Joint Stock Bank; but the Bank of England has no access to the account of the German Government at that bank; they cannot tell how much German money is lying to the credit there. Nor can the Bank of England infer much from the balance of the London Joint Stock Bank in their Bank, for the German money was probably paid in various sums to that bank, and lent out again in other various sums. It might to some extent augment that bank's balance at the Bank of England, or it might not, but it certainly would not be so much added to that balance; and inspection of that bank's balance would not enable the Bank of England to determine even in the vaguest manner what the entire sum was for which it might be asked at any moment. Nor would the inspection of the bankers' balances as a whole lead to any certain and sure conclusions. Something might be inferred from them, but not anything certain. Those balances are no doubt in a state of constant fluctuation; and very possibly during the time that the German money was coming in some other might be going out. Any sudden increase in the bankers' balances would be a probable indication of new foreign money, but new foreign money might come in without causing an increase, since some other and contemporaneous cause might effect a counteracting decrease.

This is the first, and the plainest way in which the German Government could take, and did take, money from this country; and in which it might have broken the Bank of England if it had liked. The German Government had money here and took it away, which is very easy to understand. But the Government also possessed a far greater power, of a somewhat more complex kind. It was the owner of many debts from England. A large part of the 'indemnity' was paid by France to Germany in bills on England, and the German Government, as those bills became due, acquired an unprecedented command over the market. As each bill arrived at maturity, the German Government could, if it chose, take the proceeds abroad; and it could do so in bullion, as for coinage purposes it wanted bullion. This would at first naturally cause a reduction in the bankers' balances; at least that would be its tendency. Supposing the German Government to hold bill A, a good bill, the banker at whose bank bill A was payable would have to pay it; and that would reduce his balance; and as the sum so paid would go to Germany, it would not appear to the credit of any other banker: the aggregate of the bankers' balances would thus be reduced. But this reduction would not be permanent. A banker who has to pay 100,000 L. cannot afford to reduce his balance at the Bank of England 100,000 L.; suppose that his liabilities are 2,000,000 L., and that as a rule he finds it necessary to keep at the Bank one-tenth of these liabilities, or 200,000 L., the payment of 100,000 L. would reduce his reserve to 100,000 L.; but his liabilities would be still 1,900,000 L. and therefore to keep up his tenth he would have 90,000 L. to find. His process for finding it is this: he calls in, say, a loan to the bill-brokers; and if no equal additional money is contemporaneously carried to these brokers (which in the case of a large withdrawal of foreign money is not probable), they must reduce their business and discount less. But the effect of this is to throw additional business on the Bank of England. They hold the ultimate reserve of the country, and they must discount out of it if no one else will: if they declined to do so there would be panic and collapse. As soon, therefore, as the withdrawal of the German money reduces the bankers' balances, there is a new demand on the Bank for fresh discounts to make up those balances. The drain on the Bank is twofold: first, the banking reserve is reduced by exportation of the German money, which reduces the means of the Bank of England; and then out of those reduced means the Bank of England has to make greater advances.

The same result may be arrived at more easily. Supposing any foreign Government or person to have any sort of securities which he can pledge in the market, that operation gives it, or him, a credit on some banker, and enables it, or him, to take money from the banking reserve at the Bank of England, and from the bankers' balances; and to replace the bankers' balances at their inevitable minimum, the Bank of England must lend. Every sudden demand on the country causes, in proportion to its magnitude, this peculiar effect. And this is the reason why the Bank of England ought, I think, to deal most cautiously and delicately with their banking deposits. They are the symbol of an indefinite liability: by means of them, as we see, an amount of money so great that it is impossible to assign a limit to it might be abstracted from the Bank of England. As the Bank of England lends money to keep up the bankers' balances, at their usual amount, and as by means of that usual amount whatever sum foreigners can get credit for may be taken from us, it is not possible to assign a superior limit (to use the scientific word) to the demands which by means of the bankers' balances may be made upon the Bank of England.

The result comes round to the simple point, on which this book is a commentary: the Bank of England, by the effect of a long history, holds the ultimate cash reserve of the country; whatever cash the country has to pay comes out of that reserve, and therefore the Bank of England has to pay it. And it is as the Bankers' Bank that the Bank of England has to pay it, for it is by being so that it becomes the keeper of the final cash reserve.

Some persons have been so much impressed with such considerations as these, that they have contended that the Bank of England ought never to lend the 'bankers' balances' at all, that they ought to keep them intact, and as an unused deposit. I am not sure, indeed, that I have seen that extreme form of the opinion in print, but I have often heard it in Lombard Street, from persons very influential and very qualified to judge; even in print I have seen close approximations to it. But I am satisfied that the laying down such a 'hard and fast' rule would be very dangerous; in very important and very changeable business rigid rules are apt to be often dangerous. In a panic, as has been said, the bankers' balances greatly augment. It is true the Bank of England has to lend the money by which they are filled. The banker calls in his money from the bill-broker, ceases to re-discount for that broker, or borrows on securities, or sells securities; and in one or other of these ways he causes a new demand for money which can only at such times be met from the Bank of England. Every one else is in want too. But without inquiring into the origin of the increase at panics, the amount of the bankers' deposits in fact increases very rapidly; an immense amount of unused money is at such moments often poured by them into the Bank of England. And nothing can more surely aggravate the panic than to forbid the Bank of England to lend that money. Just when money is most scarce you happen to have an unusually large fund of this particular species of money, and you should lend it as fast as you can at such moments, for it is ready lending which cures panics, and non-lending or niggardly lending which aggravates them.

At other times, particularly at the quarterly payment of the dividends, an absolute rule which laid down that the bankers' balances were never to be lent, would be productive of great inconvenience. A large sum is just then paid from the Government balance to the bankers' balances, and if you permitted the Bank to lend it while it was still in the hands of the Government, but forbad them to lend it when it came into the hands of the bankers, a great tilt upwards in the value of money would be the consequence, for a most important amount of it would suddenly have become ineffective.

But the idea that the bankers' balances ought never to be lent is only a natural aggravation of the truth that these balances ought to be used with extreme caution; that as they entail a liability peculiarly great and singularly difficult to foresee, they ought never to be used like a common deposit.

It follows from what has been said that there are always possible and very heavy demands on the Bank of England which are not shown in the account of the Banking department at all: these demands may be greatest when the liabilities shown by that account are smallest, and lowest when those liabilities are largest. If, for example, the German Government brings bills or other good securities to this market, obtains money with them, and removes that money from the market in bullion, that money may, if the German Government choose, be taken wholly from the Bank of England. If the wants of the German Government be urgent, and if the amount of gold 'arrivals,' that is, the gold coming here from the mining countries, be but small, that gold will be taken from the Bank of England, for there is no other large store in the country. The German Government is only a conspicuous example of a foreign power which happens lately to have had an unusual command of good securities, and an unusually continuous wish to use them in England. Any foreign state hereafter which wants cash will be likely to come here for it; so long as the Bank of France should continue not to pay in specie, a foreign state which wants it must of necessity come to London for it.

And no indication of the likelihood or unlikelihood of that want can be found in the books of the Bank of England.

What is almost a revolution in the policy of the Bank of England necessarily follows: no certain or fixed proportion of its liabilities can in the present times be laid down as that which the Bank ought to keep in reserve. The old notion that one-third, or any other such fraction, is in all cases enough, must be abandoned. The probable demands upon the Bank are so various in amount, and so little disclosed by the figures of the account, that no simple and easy calculation is a sufficient guide. A definite proportion of the liabilities might often be too small for the reserve, and sometimes too great. The forces of the enemy being variable, those of the defence cannot always be the same.

I admit that this conclusion is very inconvenient. In past times it has been a great aid to the Bank and to the public to be able to decide on the proper policy of the Bank from a mere inspection of its account. In that way the Bank knew easily what to do and the public knew easily what to foresee. But, unhappily, the rule which is most simple is not always the rule which is most to be relied upon. The practical difficulties of life often cannot be met by very simple rules; those dangers being complex and many, the rules for encountering them cannot well be single or simple. A uniform remedy for many diseases often ends by killing the patient.

Another simple rule often laid down for the management of the Bank of England must now be abandoned also. It has been said that the Bank of England should look to the market rate, and make its own rate conform to that. This rule was, indeed, always erroneous. The first duty of the Bank of England was to protect the ultimate cash of the country, and to raise the rate of interest so as to protect it. But this rule was never so erroneous as now, because the number of sudden demands upon that reserve was never formerly so great. The market rate of Lombard Street is not influenced by those demands. That rate is determined by the amount of deposits in the hands of bill-brokers and bankers, and the amount of good bills and acceptable securities offered at the moment. The probable efflux of bullion from the Bank scarcely affects it at all; even the real efflux affects it but little; if the open market did not believe that the Bank rate would be altered in consequence of such effluxes the market rate would not rise. If the Bank choose to let its bullion go unheeded, and is seen to be going so to choose, the value of money in Lombard Street will remain unaltered. The more numerous the demands on the Bank for bullion, and the more variable their magnitude, the more dangerous is the rule that the Bank rate of discount should conform to the market rate. In former quiet times the influence, or the partial influence, of that rule has often produced grave disasters. In the present difficult times an adherence to it is a recipe for making a large number of panics.

A more distinct view of abstract principle must be taken before we can fix on the amount of the reserve which the Bank of England ought to keep. Why should a bank keep any reserve? Because it may be called on to pay certain liabilities at once and in a moment. Why does any bank publish an account? In order to satisfy the public that it possesses cashor available securitiesenough to meet its liabilities. The object of publishing the account of the banking department of the Bank of England is to let the nation see how the national reserve of cash stands, to assure the public that there is enough and more than enough to meet not only all probable calls, but all calls of which there can be a chance of reasonable apprehension. And there is no doubt that the publication of the Bank account gives more stability to the money market than any other kind of precaution would give. Some persons, indeed, feared that the opposite result would happen; they feared that the constant publication of the incessant changes in the reserve would terrify and harass the public mind. An old banker once told me: 'Sir, I was on Lord Althorp's committee which decided on the publication of the Bank account, and I voted against it. I thought it would frighten people. But I am bound to own that the committee was right and I was wrong, for that publication has given the money market a greater sense of security than anything else which has happened in my time.' The diffusion of confidence through Lombard Street and the world is the object of the publication of the Bank accounts and of the Bank reserve.

But that object is not attained if the amount of that reserve when so published is not enough to tranquillise people. A panic is sure to be caused if that reserve is, from whatever cause, exceedingly low. At every moment there is a certain minimum which I will call the apprehension minimum,' below which the reserve cannot fall without great risk of diffused fear; and by this I do not mean absolute panic, but only a vague fright and timorousness which spreads itself instantly, and as if by magic, over the public mind. Such seasons of incipient alarm are exceedingly dangerous, because they beget the calamities they dread. What is most feared at such moments of susceptibility is the destruction of credit; and if any grave failure or bad event happens at such moments, the public fancy seizes on it, there is a general run, and credit is suspended. The Bank reserve then never ought to be diminished below the 'apprehension point.' And this is as much as to say, that it never ought very closely to approach that point; since, if it gets very near, some accident may easily bring it down to that point and cause the evil that is feared.

There is no 'royal road' to the amount of the 'apprehension minimum': no abstract argument, and no mathematical computation will teach it to us. And we cannot expect that they should. Credit is an opinion generated by circumstances and varying with those circumstances. The state of credit at any particular time is a matter of fact only to be ascertained like other matters of fact; it can only be known by trial and inquiry. And in the same way, nothing but experience can tell us what amount of 'reserve' will create a diffused confidence; on such a subject there is no way of arriving at a just conclusion except by incessantly watching the public mind, and seeing at each juncture how it is affected.

Of course in such a matter the cardinal rule to be observed is, that errors of excess are innocuous but errors of defect are destructive. Too much reserve only means a small loss of profit, but too small a reserve may mean 'ruin.' Credit may be at once shaken, and if some terrifying accident happen to supervene, there may be a run on the Banking department that may be too much for it, as in 1857 and 1866, and may make it unable to pay its way without assistanceas it was m those years.

And the observance of this maxim is the more necessary because the 'apprehension minimum' is not always the same. On the contrary, in times when the public has recently seen the Bank of England exposed to remarkable demands, it is likely to expect that such demands may come again. Conspicuous and recent events educate it, so to speak; it expects that much will be demanded when much has of late often been demanded, and that little will be so, when in general but little has been so. A bank like the Bank of England must always, therefore, be on the watch for a rise, if I may so express it, in the apprehension minimum; it must provide an adequate fund not only to allay the misgivings of to-day, but also to allay what may be the still greater misgivings of to-morrow. And the only practical mode of obtaining this object is--to keep the actual reserve always in advance of the minimum 'apprehension' reserve.

And this involves something much more. As the actual reserve is never to be less, and is always, if possible, to exceed by a reasonable amount the 'minimum' apprehension reserve, it must when the Bank is quiet and taking no precautions very considerably exceed that minimum. All the precautions of the Bank take time to operate. The principal precaution is a rise in the rate of discount, and such a rise certainly does attract money from the Continent and from all the world much faster than could have been anticipated. But it does not act instantaneously; even the right rate, the ultimately attractive rate, requires an interval for its action, and before the money can come here. And the right rate is often not discovered for some time. It requires several 'moves,' as the phrase goes, several augmentations of the rate of discount by the Bank, before the really effectual rate is reached, and in the mean time bullion is ebbing away and the 'reserve' is diminishing. Unless, therefore, in times without precaution the actual reserve exceed the 'apprehension minimum' by at least the amount which may be taken away in the inevitable interval, and before the available precautions begin to operate, the rule prescribed will be infringed, and the actual reserve will be less than the 'apprehension' minimum. In time the precautions taken may attract gold and raise the reserve to the needful amount, but in the interim the evils may happen against which the rule was devised, diffused apprehension may arise, and then any unlucky accident may cause many calamities.

I may be asked, 'What does all this reasoning in practice come to? At the present moment how much reserve do you say the Bank of England should keep? state your recommendation clearly (I know it will be said) if you wish to have it attended to.' And I will answer the question plainly, though in so doing there is a great risk that the principles I advocate may be in some degree injured through some mistake I may make in applying them.

I should say that at the present time the mind of the monetary world would become feverish and fearful if the reserve in the Banking department of the Bank of England went below 10,000,000 L. Estimated by the idea of old times, by the idea even of ten years ago, that sum, I know, sounds extremely large. My own nerves were educated to smaller figures, because I was trained in times when the demands on us were less, when neither was so much reserve wanted nor did the public expect so much. But I judge from such observations as I can make of the present state of men's minds, that in fact, and whether justifiably or not, the important and intelligent part of the public which watches the Bank reserve becomes anxious and dissatisfied if that reserve falls below 10,000,000 L. That sum, therefore, I call the 'apprehension minimum' for the present times. Circumstances may change and may make it less or more, but according to the most careful estimate I can make, that is what I should call it now.

It will be said that this estimate is arbitrary and these figures are conjectures. I reply that I only submit them for the judgment of others. The main question is one of fact--Does not the public mind begin to be anxious and timorous just where I have placed the apprehension point? and the deductions from that are comparatively simple questions of mixed fact and reasoning. The final appeal in such cases necessarily is to those who are conversant with and who closely watch the facts.

I shall perhaps be told also that a body like the Court of the Directors of the Bank of England cannot act on estimates like these: that such a body must have a plain rule and keep to it. I say in reply, that if the correct framing of such estimates is necessary for the good guidance of the Bank, we must make a governing body which can correctly frame such estimates. We must not suffer from a dangerous policy because we have inherited an imperfect form of administration. I have before explained in what manner the government of the Bank of England should, I consider, be strengthened, and that government so strengthened would, I believe, be altogether competent to a wise policy.

Then I should say, putting the foregoing reasoning into figures, that the Bank ought never to keep less than 11,000,000 L.. or 11,500,000 L. since experience shows that a million, or a million and a half, may be taken from us at any time. I should regard this as the practical minimum at which, roughly of course, the Bank should aim, and which it should try never to be below. And, in order not to be below 11,500,000

L., the Bank must begin to take precautions when the reserve is between 14,000,000 L. and 15,000,000 l.; for experience shows that between 2,000,000 L. and 3,000,000 L. may, probably enough, be withdrawn from the Bank store before the right rate of interest is found which will attract money from abroad, and before that rate has had time to attract it. When the reserve is between 14,000,000 L. and 15,000,000 L., and when it begins to be diminished by foreign demand, the Bank of England should, I think, begin to act, and to raise the rate of interest.

CHAPTER XIII.

Conclusion.

I know it will be said that in this work I have pointed out a deep malady, and only suggested a superficial remedy. I have tediously insisted that the natural system of banking is that of many banks keeping their own cash reserve, with the penalty of failure before them if they neglect it. I have shown that our system is that of a single bank keeping the whole reserve under no effectual penalty of failure. And yet I propose to retain that system, and only attempt to mend and palliate it.

I can only reply that I propose to retain this system because I am quite sure that it is of no manner of use proposing to alter it. A system of credit which has slowly grown up as years went on, which has suited itself to the course of business, which has forced itself on the habits of men, will not be altered because theorists disapprove of it, or because books are written against it. You might as well, or better, try to alter the English monarchy and substitute a republic, as to alter the present constitution of the English money market, founded on the Bank of England, and substitute for it a system in which each bank shall keep its own reserve. There is no force to be found adequate to so vast a reconstruction, and so vast a destructions and therefore it is useless proposing them.

No one who has not long considered the subject can have a notion how much this dependence on the Bank of England is fixed in our national habits. I have given so many illustrations in this book that I fear I must have exhausted my reader's patience, but I will risk giving another. I suppose almost everyone thinks that our system of savings' banks is sound and good. Almost everyone would be surprised to hear that there is any possible objection to it. Yet see what it amounts to. By the last return the savings' banks--the old and the Post Office together-- contain about 60,000,000 L. of deposits, and against this they hold in the funds securities of the best kind. But they hold no cash whatever. They have of course the petty cash about the various branches necessary for daily work. But of cash in ultimate reserve cash in reserve against a panicthe savings' banks have not a sixpence. These banks depend on being able in a panic to realise their securities. But it has been shown over and over again, that in a panic such securities can only be realised by the help of the Bank of Englandthat it is only the Bank with the ultimate cash reserve which has at such moments any new money, or any power to lend and act. If in a general panic there were a run on the savings' banks, those banks could not sell 100,000 L. of Consols without the help of the Bank of England; not holding themselves a cash reserve for times of panic, they are entirely dependent on the one Bank which does hold that reserve.

This is only a single additional instance beyond the innumerable ones given, which shows how deeply our system of banking is fixed in our ways of thinking. The Government keeps the money of the poor upon it, and the nation fully approves of their doing so. No one hears a syllable of objection. And every practical manevery man who knows the scene of actionwill agree that our system of banking, based on a single reserve in the Bank of England, cannot be altered, or a system of many banks, each keeping its own reserve, be substituted for it. Nothing but a revolution would effect it, and there is nothing to cause a revolution.

This being so, there is nothing for it but to make the best of our banking system, and to work it in the best way that it is capable of. We can only use palliatives, and the point is to get the best palliative we can. I have endeavoured to show why it seems to me that the palliatives which I have suggested are the best that are at our disposal.

I have explained why the French plan will not suit our English world. The direct appointment of the Governor and Deputy-Governor of the Bank of England by the executive Government would not lessen our evils or help our difficulties. I fear it would rather make both worse. But possibly it may be suggested that I ought to explain why the American system, or some modification, would not or might not be suitable to us. The American law says that each national bank shall have a fixed proportion of cash to its liabilities (there are two classes of banks, and two different proportions; but that is not to the present purpose), and it ascertains by inspectors, who inspect at their own times, whether the required amount of cash is in the bank or not. It may be asked, could nothing like this be attempted in England? could not it, or some modification, help us out of our difficulties? As far as the American banking system is one of many reserves, I have said why I think it is of no use considering whether we should adopt it or not. We cannot adopt it if we would. The one-reserve system is fixed upon us. The only practical imitation of the American system would be to enact that the Banking department of the Bank of England should always keep a fixed proportionsay one-third of its liabilitiesin reserve. But, as we have seen before, a fixed proportion of the liabilities, even when that proportion is voluntarily chosen by the directors, and not imposed by law, is not the proper standard for a bank reserve. Liabilities may be imminent or distant, and a fixed rule which imposes the same reserve for both will sometimes err by excess, and sometimes by defect. It will waste profits by over-provision against ordinary danger, and yet it may not always save the bank; for this provision is often likely enough to be insufficient against rare and unusual dangers. But bad as is this system when voluntarily chosen, it becomes far worse when legally and compulsorily imposed. In a sensitive state of the English money market the near approach to the legal limit of reserve would be a sure incentive to panic; if one-third were fixed by law, the moment the banks were close to one-third, alarm would begin, and would run like magic. And the fear would be worse because it would not be unfoundedat least, not wholly. If you say that the Bank shall always hold one-third of its liabilities as a reserve, you say in fact that this one-third shall always be useless, for out of it the Bank cannot make advances, cannot give extra help, cannot do what we have seen the holders of the ultimate reserve ought to do and must do. There is no help for us in the American system; its very essence and principle are faulty.

We must therefore, I think, have recourse to feeble and humble palliatives such as I have suggested. With good sense, good judgment, and good care, I have no doubt that they may be enough. But I have written in vain if I require to say now that the problem is delicate, that the solution is varying and difficult, and that the result is inestimable to us all.

APPENDIX.

Note A.

Liabilities and Cash Reserve of the Chief Banking Systems.

The following is a comparison of the liabilities to the public, and of the cash reserve, of the banking systems of the United Kingdom, France, Germany, and the United States. For the United Kingdom the figures are the most defective, as they only include the deposits of the Bank of England, and of the London joint stock banks, and the banking reserve of the Bank of England, which is the only cash available against these liabilities is also the only cash reserve against the similar liabilities of the London private banks, the provincial English banks, and the Scotch and Irish banks. In the case of England, therefore, the method of comparison exhibits a larger proportion of cash to liabilities than what really exists.

(1) ENGLISH BANKING.

Liabilities.
Deposits of Bank of England, less estimated Joint Stock Bank balances, at December 31, 1872 L 29,000,000

Deposits of London Joint Stock Banks at December 31 1872 (see 'Economist,' February 8, 1873) L 91,000,000 Total liabilities L 120,000,000

Reserve of Cash Banking Reserve in Bank of England. L 13,500,000

Making proportion of cash reserve to liabilities to the public about 11'2 per cent.

(2) BANK of FRANCE (FEBRUARY, 1873).

Liabilities
Circulation L 110,000,000
Deposits L 15,000,000
Total liabilities L 125,000,000

Reserve of Cash.

Coin and bullion in hand L 32,000,000

Making proportion of cash reserve to liabilities to the public about 25 per cent.

(3) BANKS OF GERMANY (JANUARY, 1873).

Liabilities

Circulation	L 63,000,000
Deposits	L 8,000,000
Acceptances and Indorsements	L 17,000,000
Total liabilities	L 88,000,000

Reserves of Cash

Cash in Hand L 41,000,000

Making proportion of cash reserve to liabilities to the public about per cent.

(4) NATIONAL BANKS OF UNITED STATES (OCTOBER 3, 1872).

Liabilities

Circulation L   67,000,000
Deposits L 145,000,000
Total liabilities L 212,000,000

Reserve of Cash

Coin and legal tenders in hand L 26,000,000

Making proportion of cash reserve to liabilities to the public about 12.3 per cent.

SUMMARY

Bank of England and London

	Liabilities to the public	Cash held	Proportion of cash to liabilities per cent
Joint Stock Banks	20,000,000	13,500,000	11.2
Bank of France	125,000,000	32,000,000	25.0
Banks of Germany	88,000,000	41,000,000	47.0
National Banks of United States	212,000,000	26,000,000	12.3

Note B.

Extract from Evidence Given by Mr. Alderman Salomons before House of Commons Select Committee in 1858

1146. [Chairman.] The effect upon yourselves of the pressure in November was, I presume, to induce you to increase your reserve in your own hands, and also to increase your deposits with the Bank of England?--Yes, that was so; but I wish to tell the Committee that that was done almost entirely by allowing the bills of exchange which we held to mature, and not by raising any money, or curtailing our accommodation to our customers. Perhaps it may be interesting to the Committee to know that on the 11th of November we held discounted bills for brokers to the amount of 5,623,000 L. Out of those bills, 2,800,000 L. matured between the 11th of November and the 4th of December, and 2,000,000 L. more between the 4th of December and the 31st. So that about 5,000,000 L. of bills matured between the 11th of November and the 31st of December; consequently we were prepared, merely by the maturing of our bills of exchange, for any demands that might possibly come upon us.

1147. I understand you to say that you did not withdraw your usual accommodation from your own customers, but that you ceased to have in deposit with the bill-brokers so large a sum of money as you had before?--Not exactly that; the bills which we had discounted were allowed to mature, and we discounted less; we kept a large reserve of cash.

1148. That is to say, you withdrew from the commercial world a part of that accommodation which you had previously given, and at the same time you increased your deposits with the Bank of England?--Yes, our deposits with the Bank of England were increased. We did not otherwise withdraw accommodation.

1149. [Mr. Weguelin.] Had you any money at call with the billbrokers?--A small amount; perhaps about 500,000 L. or less, which we did not call in.

1150. [Chairman.] What I understand you to say is, that the effect of the commercial pressure upon you was to induce you upon the whole to withdraw from commerce an amount of accommodation which in other times you had given, and at the same time to increase your deposits with the Bank of England?--So far only as ceasing to discount with strangers, persons not having current accounts with us.

1151. Or to give the same amount to the bill-broker?--For a while, instead of discounting for brokers and strangers, we allowed our bills to mature, and remained quiescent with a view to enable us to meet any demand that might be made on ourselves.

1152. Except what you felt bound to your own customers to continue to give, you ceased to make advances?--Quite so; perhaps I might say at the same time, that besides a large balance which we kept at the Bank of England, which of course was as available as in our own tills, we increased our notes in our tills at the head office and at all the branches.

1153. I suppose at that time large sales of public securities were made by the London joint stock banks, which securities were purchased by the public?--It is understood that some joint stock and other banks sold, but I believe it is quite certain that the public purchased largely, because they always purchase when the funds fall.

1154. Are you prepared to give the Committee any opinion of your own as to the effect, one way or the other, which the system of the joint stock banks may have produced with regard to aggravating or diminishing the commercial pressure in the autumn of last year?--I should state, generally, that the joint stock banks, as well as all other banks, in London, by collecting money from those who had it to spare, must of necessity have assisted, and could not do otherwise than assist commerce, both then and at all other times.

1155. You say that your discounts, either at your own counter or through the bill-brokers, are ordinarily very large, but that at the time of severest pressure you contracted them so far as you thought was just to your own immediate customers?--Yes; but the capital was still there, because it was at the Bank of England, and it was capable of being used for short periods; if we did not want it, others might have used it.

1156. [Mr. Weguelin.] In fact, it was used by the Bank of England?-- Undoubtedly; I should suppose so; there is no question about it.

1157. You, of course, felt quite certain that your deposits in the Bank of England might be had upon demand?--We had no doubt about it.

1158 You did not take into consideration the effect of the law of 1844, which might have placed the Banking Department of the Bank of England in such a position as not to be able to meet the demands of its depositors? I must say that that never gave us the smallest concern.

1159. You therefore considered that, if the time should arrive, the Government would interfere with some measure as they had previously done to enable the Bank to meet the demands upon it?--We should always have thought that if the Bank of England had stopped payment, all the machinery of Government would have stopped with it, and we never could have believed that so formidable a calamity would have arisen if the Government could have prevented it.

1160. [Chairman.] The notion of the convertibility of the note being in danger never crossed your mind?--Never for a moment; nothing of the kind.

1161. [Mr. Weguelin.] I refer not to the convertibility of the note, but to the state of the Banking Department of the Bank of England?--If we had thought that there was any doubt whatever about it, we should have taken our bank-notes and put them in our own strong chest. We could never for a moment believe an event of that kind as likely to happen.

1162. Therefore you think that the measure taken by the Government, of issuing a letter authorising the Bank of England to increase their issues of notes upon securities, was what was generally expected by the commercial world, and what in future the commercial world would look to in such a conjunction of circumstances?--We looked for some measure of that nature. That, no doubt, was the most obvious one. We had great doubts whether it would come when it did, until the very last moment.

1163. Have you ever contemplated the possibility of the Bank refusing to advance, under circumstances similar to those which existed in November, 1857, upon good banking securities?--Of course I have, and it is a very difficult question to answer as to what its effect might be; but the notion appears to me to be so thoroughly ingrained in the minds of the commercial world, that whenever you have good security it ought to be convertible at the Bank in some shape or way, that I have very great doubt indeed whether the Bank can ever take a position to refuse to assist persons who have good commercial securities to offer.

1164. [Mr. Cayley.] When you say that you have come to some fresh arrangement with regard to your allowance of interest upon deposits, do you speak of yourselves as the London and Westminster Bank, or of some of the other banks in combination with yourselves?--I think all the banks have come to an understanding that it is not desirable, either for their proprietors or for the public, to follow closely at all times the alterations of the Bank. I believe it is understood amongst them all that they do not intend following that course in future.

1165. Is that from a feeling that it is rather dangerous under particular circumstances?--I cannot admit as to its being dangerous, but there can be no doubt of this, that there is a notion in the public mind which we ought not to contend against, that when you offer a high rate of interest for money, you rather do it because you want the person's money, than because you are obeying the market rate; and I think it is desirable that we should show that if persons wish to employ their money, and want an excessive rate, they may take it away and employ it themselves.

1166. You think that there is now a general understanding amongst the banks which you have mentioned, to act upon a different principle from that on which they acted during last October and November?--I think I may say that I know that to be the case.

1167. Was not it the fact that this system of giving so high a rate of interest upon money at call commenced very much with the establishment of some banks during the last year or two, which, instead of demanding 10 days' or a month's notice, were willing to allow interest upon only three days' notice; did not that system begin about two years ago?--I do not think it began with the new banks; I think it began with one of the older banks; I know that as regards my own bank, that we were forced into it; I forgot to say, that with regard to ourselves in taking money on deposit, the parties must leave the money a month, or they lose interest. We do not take money from any depositor at interest unless upon the understand ing and condition that it remains a month with us; he may withdraw it within the month, but then he forfeits interest; it will not carry interest unless it is with us a month, and then it is removable on demand without notice.

1168. Is it or is it not a fact that some of the banks pay interest upon their current accounts?--Yes, I think most of the new banks do so; and the Unlon Bank of London does it.

1169. At a smaller rate than upon their deposits, I presume?--I think at a smaller rate, but I believe it is a fixed rate on the minimum balance for some period, either six months or one month, I do not exactly know the period. I think I ought to add (and I believe it is the case with all the banks) that the London and Westminster Bank, from the day of its first institution until the present day, has never re-discounted a bill. No bill has ever left our bank unless it has been for payment.

1170. Is not that generally the case with the London joint stock banks?--I believe it is the case.

1171. [Mr. Weguelin.] But you sometimes lend money upon bills deposited with you by bill-brokers?--Yes.

1172. And you occasionally call in that money and re-deliver those securities?--Yes; but that we do to a very small extent.

1173. Is not that equivalent to a re-discount of bills?--No; the discount of a bill and the lending money on bills are very different things. When we discount a bill, that bill becomes our property; it is in our control, and we keep it and lock it up until it falls due; but when brokers come to us and want to borrow, say 50,000 L. on a deposit of bills, and we let them have the money and afterwards return those bills to them and we get back our money, surely that is not a re-discount.

1174. When you want to employ your money for a short period, do you not frequently take bills of long date, and advance upon them?--But that is not a re-discount on our part. Very often brokers in borrowing money send in bills of long date, and afterwards we call in that loan; but that is no more a re-discount than lending money upon consols and calling in that money again. It is not an advance of ours; we do not seek it; they come to us and borrow our money, and give us a security; when we want our money we call for that money, and return their security. Surely that is not a re-discount.

1175. [Mr. Hankey.] Is there not this clear distinction between returning a bill on which you have made an advance and discounting a bill, that if you have discounted a bill your liability continues upon the bill until that bill has come to maturity?--Yes.

1176. In the other case you have no further liability whatever?--Certamly.

1177. Should you not consider that a very important distinction?--I think it is an important distinction. Take this case: suppose a party comes to us and borrows 50,000 L., and we lend it him, and when the loan becomes due we take our money back again. Surely that is not a discount on our part.

1178. Is there not this distinction, that if you re-discount you may go on pledging the liability of your bank to an almost unlimited amount, whereas in the other case you only get back that money which you have lent?--Undoubtedly.

1179. [Mr. Cayley.] The late Chancellor of the Exchequer stated before the adjournment, in a speech in the House of Commons, that during the Monday, Tuesday, Wednesday, and Thursday of the panic, the Bank was almost, if not entirely, the only body that discounted commercial bills; how can you reconcile that with what you have said, that you gave as much accommodation as usual to your customers?--I am not responsible for what the Chancellor of the Exchequer said; I am responsible for what I am now stating as to the course of our bank, that our advances to our customers on the 31st of December were nearly 500,000 L. higher than they were on the 1st of October. With regard to our not discounting for other parties, it was in consequence of the discredit which prevailed, that it was necessary we should hold a portion of our deposits in order that they should be available in case persons called for them; a certain number of persons did so; in the month of November we had a reduction of our deposits, and if we had gone on discounting for brokers we should have had to go into the market ourselves to raise money on our Government securities, but we avoided that by not discounting, and leaving our money at the Bank of England.

1180. Then you did not discount as much as usual for your customers during that period?--Yes. we did, and more.

1181. But not to strangers?--Not to strangers; I make a distinction between our transactions with our customers, who of course expect us to give accommodation, and discounts for brokers, which is entirely voluntary, depending upon our having money to employ.

1182. How would it have been if the letter had not issued at the last moment? That is a question which I can hardly answer.

1183. What do you mean by that general expression of yours?--It is impossible to predicate what may happen in time of panic and alarm. A great alarm prevailed certainly amongst the commercial world, and it could never have been alleviated, except by some extraordinary means of relief. We might probably have been in the state in which Hamburg was, where they have no bank-notes in circulation.

1184. [Mr. Spooner.] What did you mean by the expression, 'the last moment'? You said that the letter came out at the last moment; the last moment of what?--It was late in the day; it was a day of great distress. For two days there was a great deal of anxiety, and everybody expected that there would be some relief; and it was when expectation, I suppose, was highly excited that the letter came, and it gave relief.

1185. Cannot you tell us what your opinion would have been, if that last moment had happened to have elapsed, and the letter had not come?--It is very difficult to say; it is too much to say that it could not have been got over. There can be no doubt whatever that what created the difficulty existed out of London, and not in it; and therefore it is much more difficult for me to give an opinion. I believe that the banking interest, both private and joint stock, was in a perfectly sound condition, and able to bear any strain which might have been brought upon it in London.

1186. [Mr. Hankey.] Can you give the Committee any idea as to what proportion of deposits you consider generally desirable to keep in reserve?--You must be very much guided by circumstances. In times of alarm, when there are failures, of course all bankers strengthen their reserves; our reserve then is larger. In times of ordinary business we find, both as regards our deposits at interest as well as those which are not at interest, that there is a constant circulation; that the receipts of money very nearly meet the payments.

1187. You probably keep at all times a certain amount of your deposits totally unemployed; in reserve?--Yes.

1188. In a normal state of commercial affairs, is there any fixed proportion, or can you give the Committee any idea of what you would consider about a fair and desirable proportion which should be so kept unemployed?--I think the best idea which I can give upon that subject is to give our annual statement, or balance sheet, for the 31st of December.

1189. Does that show what amount of unemployed money you had on that day?--Yes. I will put in a statement, which perhaps will be the best means of meeting the question, showing the cash in hand on the 30th of June and the 31st of December in every year, as shown by our published accounts, together with our money at call and our Government securities; that will be perhaps the best and most convenient way of giving the information you desire to have. (See Table below.)

1190. Do you consider that when your deposits are materially on the increase it is necessary to keep a larger amount of money in reserve than you would keep at other times?--I may say that, as a general rule, our reserve would always bear some proportion to our deposits.

1191. Do you employ your money in the discounting of bills for other persons than your own customers?--Discount brokers.

1192. Only to discount brokers? Yes.

1193. Not to strangers who are in the habit of bringing you in bills; commercial houses?--I should say generally not. We have one or two houses for whom we discount who have not accounts with us as bankers, but generally we do not discount except for our customers or for billbrokers.

1194. Do you consider that any advantage can arise to the public by the Bank of England advancing to a greater extent than can be considered strictly prudent on the soundest principle of banking, under the idea of their affording aid to the commercial world?--As I said before, as long as there are good bills in circulation, that is, bills about which there would be no doubt of their being paid at maturity, there should be some means by which those bills could be discounted.

1195. And do you think that it is part of the functions of the Bank of England to discount a bill for anybody, merely because the party holding the bill wishes to convert it into cash?--As I said before, the Bank of England will have great difficulty in getting rid of that inconvenient idea which there is in the mind of the public, that the Bank of England is something more than an ordinary joint stock bank. I think it must depend very much upon circumstances whether you can or cannot refuse the discount of good bills which are offered to you.

Note C.

Statement of Circulation and Deposits of the Bank of Dundee at Intervals of Ten Years between 1764 and 1864.

Year	Circulation	Deposits
1764	30,395	–
1774	27,670	–
1784	56,342	–
1794	50,354	–
1804	54,096	157,821
1814	46,627	445,066
1824	29,675	343,948
1834	26,467	563,202
1844	27,504	535,253
1854	40,774	705,222
1864	41,118	684,898

The Bank did not begin to receive deposits until 1792, in which year they amounted to 35,9441.

Note D.

Meeting of the Proprietors of the Bank of England.

September 13, 1866.

(From 'Economist,' September 22, 1866.)

A General Court of the Bank of England was held at the Bank at twelve o'clock on the 3th instant, for the purpose of declaring a dividend for the past half-year.

Mr. Launcelot Holland, the Governor of the Bank, who presided upon the occasion, addressed the proprietors as follows: This is one of the quarterly general courts appointed by our charter, and it is also one of our half-yearly general courts, held under our bye-laws, for the purpose of declaring a dividend. From a statement which I hold in my hand it appears that the net profits of the Bank for the half-year ending on the 31st of August last amounted to 970,014 L. 17s. 10d.; making the amount of the rest on that day, 3,981,783 L. 18s. 11d.; and after providing for a dividend at the rate of 6 L. 10s. per cent, the rest will stand at 3,035,838 L.. 18s. 11d. The court of directors, therefore, propose that a half-yearly dividend of interest and profits, to the amount of 6 L. 10s. per cent, without deduction on account of income tax, shall be made on the 10th of October next. That is the proposal I have now to lay before the general court; but as important events have occurred since we last met, I think it right I should briefly advert to them upon this occasion. A great strain has within the last few months been put upon the resources of this house, and of the whole banking community of London; and I think I am entitled to say that not only this house but the entire banking body acquitted themselves most honourably and creditably throughout that very trying period. Banking is a very peculiar business, and it depends so much upon credit that the least blast of suspicion is sufficient to sweep away, as it were, the harvest of a whole year. But the manner in which the banking establishments generally of London met the demands made upon them during the greater portion of the past half-year affords a most satisfactory proof of the soundness of the principles on which their business is conducted. This house exerted itself to the utmost--and exerted itself most successfully--to meet the crisis. We did not flinch from our post. When the storm came upon us, on the morning on which it became known that the house of Overend and Co. had failed, we were in as sound and healthy a position as any banking establishment could hold; and on that day and throughout the succeeding week, we made advances which would hardly be credited. I do not believe that any one would have thought of predicting, even at the shortest period beforehand, the greatness of those advances. It was not unnatural that in this state of things a certain degree of alarm should have taken possession of the public mind, and that those who required accommodation from the Bank should have gone to the Chancellor of the Exchequer and requested the Government to empower us to issue notes beyond the statutory amount, if we should think that such a measure was desirable. But we had to act before we could receive any such power, and before the Chancellor of the Exchequer was perhaps out of his bed we had advanced one-half of our reserves, which were certainly thus reduced to an amount which we could not witness without regret. But we could not flinch from the duty which we conceived was imposed upon us of supporting the banking community, and I am not aware that any legitimate application for assistance made to this house was refused. Every gentleman who came here with adequate security was liberally dealt with, and if accommodation could not be afforded to the full extent which was demanded, no one who offered proper security failed to obtain relief from this house. I have perhaps gone a little more into details than is customary upon these occasions, but the times have been unusually interesting, and I thought it desirable to say this much in justification of the course adopted by this house of running its balances down to a point which some gentlemen may consider dangerous. Looking back, however, upon recent events, I cannot take any blame to this court for not having been prepared for such a tornado as that which burst upon us on the ith of May; and I hope the court of proprietors will feel that their directors acted properly upon that occasion, and that they did their best to meet a very extraordinary state of circumstances. I have now only to move that a dividend be declared at the rate of 6 L. 10s. per cent for the past half-year.

Mr. Hyam said that before the question was put he wished to offer a few observations to the court. He believed that the statement of accounts which had just been laid before them was perfectly satisfactory. He also thought that the directors had done their best to assist the commercial classes throughout the late monetary crisis; but it appeared to him at the same time that they were in fault in not having applied at an earlier period to the Chancellor of the Exchequer for a suspension of the Bank Act. It was well known that the demand on the Bank was materially lessened in the earlier part of the day, in consequence of a rumour which had been extensively circulated that permission to overstep the limits laid down in the Act had been granted. That concession, however, had only been made after the most urgent representations had been addressed to the Chancellor of the Exchequer at a late hour in the night, and if it had then been refused he felt persuaded that the state of affairs would have been much worse on the Saturday than it had been on the Friday. The fact was that the Act of 1844 was totally unsuited to the present requirements of the country, which since that period had tripled or quadrupled its commerce; and he was sorry to know that the measure seemed to meet with the approval of many of their directors. Any one who read the speeches made in the course of the discussion on Mr. Watkins' motion must see that the subject called for further inquiry; and he trusted that the demand for that inquiry would yet be conceded.

Mr. Jones said he entirely dissented from the views with respect to the Bank Act entertained by the hon. proprietor who had just addressed the court. In his opinion the main cause of the recent monetary crisis was that, while we had bought 275,000,000 L. worth of foreign produce in the year 1865, the value of our exports had only been 165,000,000 L., so that we had a balance against us to the amount of 110,000,000 L. He believed that the Bank acted wisely in resisting every attempt to increase the paper currency, and he felt convinced that the working classes would be the people least likely to benefit by the rise in prices which would take place under such a change.

Mr. Moxon said he should be glad to know what was the amount of bad debts made by the Bank during the past half-year. It was stated very confidently out of doors that during that period the directors had between 3,000,000 L. and 4,000,000 L. of bills returned to them.

The Governor of the Bank.--May I ask what is your authority for that statement? We are rather amused at hearing it, and we have never been able to trace any rumour of the kind to an authentic source.

Mr. Moxon continued--Whether the bad debts were large or small, he thought it was desirable that they should all know what was their actual amount. They had been told at their last meeting that the Bank held a great many railway debentures; and he should like to know whether any of those debentures came from railway companies that had since been unable to meet their obligations. He understood that a portion of their property was locked up in advances made on account of the Thames Embankment, and in other ways which did not leave the money available for general banking and commercial purposes; and if that were so, he should express his disapproval of such a policy. There was another important point to which he wished to advert. He was anxious to know what was the aggregate balance of the joint stock banks in the Bank of England. He feared that some time or other the joint stock banks would be in a position to command perhaps the stoppage of the Bank of England. If that were not so, the sooner the public were full & informed upon the point the better. But if ten or twelve joint stock banks had large balances in the Bank of England, and if the Bank balances were to run very low, people would naturally begin to suspect that the joint stock banks had more power over the Bank of England than they ought to have. He wished further to ask whether the directors had of late taken into consideration the expediency of paying interest on deposits. He believed that under their present mode of carrying on their business they were foregoing large profits which they might receive with advantage to themselves and to the public; and he would recommend that they should undertake the custody of securities after the system adopted by the Bank of France. In conclusion, he proposed to move three resolutions, for the purpose of providing, first, that a list of all the proprietors of Bank stock should be printed, with a separate entry of the names of all those persons not entitled to vote from the smallness of their stock, or from the shortness of time during which they held it; secondly, that a copy of the charter of the Bank, with the rules, orders, and bye-laws passed for the good government of their corporation, should be printed for the use of the shareholders; and thirdly, that auditors should be appointed to make detailed audits of their accounts.

Mr. Gerstenberg recommended that the directors should take some step for the purpose of preventing the spread of such erroneous notions as that which lately prevailed on the Continent, that the Bank was about to suspend specie payments.

Mr. W. Botly said he wished to see the directors taking into their consideration the expediency of allowing interest on deposits.

Mr. Alderman Salomons said he wished to take that opportunity of stating that he believed nothing could be more satisfactory to the managers and shareholders of joint stock banks than the testimony which the Governor of the Bank of England had that day borne to the sound and honourable manner in which their business was conducted. It was mainfestly desirable that the joint stock banks and the banking interest generally should work in harmony with the Bank of England; and he sincerely thanked the Governor of the Bank for the kindly manner in which he had alluded to the mode in which the joint stock banks had met the late monetary crisis.

The Governor of the Bank said--Before putting the question for the declaration of a dividend, I wish to refer to one or two points that have been raised by the gentlemen who have addressed the court on this occasion. The most prominent topic brought under our notice is the expediency of allowing interest on deposits; and upon that point I must say that I believe a more dangerous innovation could not be made in the practice of the Bank of England. The downfall of Overend and Gurney, and of many other houses, must be traced to the policy which they adopted of paying interest on deposits at call, while they were themselves tempted to invest the money so received in speculations in Ireland or in America, or at the bottom of the sea, where it was not available when a moment of pressure arrived.

Mr. Botly said he did not mean deposits on call.

The Governor of the Bank of England continued--That is only a matter of detail; the main question is whether we ought to pay interest on deposits, and of such policy I must express my entire disapproval. Mr. Moxon has referred to the amount of our debts, but, as I stated when I took the liberty of interrupting him, we could never trace the origin of any rumour which prevailed upon that subject. As far as it can be said to have ever existed it had its origin most probably in the vast amount advanced by the Bank. It must, however, be remembered that we did not make our advances without ample security, and the best proof of that is the marvelously small amount of bad debts which we contracted. It has never been a feature of the Bank to state what was the precise amount of those debts; but I believe that if I were to mention it upon the present occasion, it would be found to be so inconsiderable that I should hardly obtain credence for the announcement I should have to make. I am convmced that our present dividend has been as honestly and as hardly earned as any that we have ever realised; but it has been obtained by means of great vigilance and great anxiety on the part of each and all of your directors; and I will add that I believe you would only diminish their sense of responsibility, and introduce confusion into the management of your business, if you were to transfer to auditors the making up of your ac counts. If your directors deserve your confidence they are surely capable of performing that duty, and if they do not deserve it you ought not to continue them in their present office. With regard to the supposed lock-up of our capital, I must observe that, with 14,000,000 L. on our hands, we must necessarily invest it in a variety of securities; but there is no ground for imagining that our money is locked up and is not available for the purpose of making commercial advances. We advanced in the space of three months the sum of 45,000,000 L.; and what more than that do you want? It has been recommended that we should take charge of securities; but we have found it necessary to refuse all securities except those of our customers; and I believe the custody of securities is becoming a growing evil. With regard to railway debentures, I do not believe we have one of a doubtful character. We have no debentures except those of first-class railway companies and companies which we know are acting within their Parliamentary limits. Having alluded to those subjects, I will now put the motion for the declaration of the dividend.

The motion was accordingly put and unanimously adopted.

The chairman then announced that that resolution should be confirmed by ballot on Tuesday next, inasmuch as the Bank could not, under the provisions of its Act of Parliament, declare otherwise than in that form a dividend higher than that which it had distributed during the preceding half-year.

The three resolutions proposed by Mr. Moxon were then read; but they were not put to the meeting, inasmuch as they found no seconders.

Mr. Alderman Salomons said that their Governor had observed that he thought the payment of interests on deposits was objectionable; and everyone must see that such a practice ought not to be adopted by the Bank of England. But he took it for granted that the Governor did not mean that his statement should apply to joint stock banks which he had himself told them had conducted their business so creditably and so successfully.

The Governor of the Bank said that what he stated was that such a system would be dangerous for the Bank of England, and dangerous if carried into effect in the way contemplated by Mr. Moxon.

Mr. P. N. Laurie said he understood the Governor of the Bank to say that it would be dangerous to take deposits on call, and in that opinion he concurred.

Mr. Alderman Salomons said that he, too, was of the same opinion.

On the motion of Mr. Alderman Salomons, seconded by Mr. Botly, a vote of thanks was passed to the Governor and the directors for their able and successful management of the Bank during the past half-year, and the proceedings then terminated.

End of The Project Gutenberg Etext of Lombard Street: A Description of the Money Market by Walter Bagehot

Made in the USA
Lexington, KY
31 July 2011